# INTERCOUNTRY INCOME DISTRIBUTION
# AND TRANSNATIONAL ENTERPRISES

# Intercountry Income Distribution and Transnational Enterprises

by

CONSTANTINE V. VAITSOS

CLARENDON PRESS · OXFORD

1974

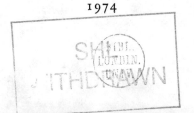

*Oxford University Press, Ely House, London W.1*

GLASGOW NEW YORK TORONTO MELBOURNE WELLINGTON
CAPE TOWN IBADAN NAIROBI DAR ES SALAAM LUSAKA ADDIS ABABA
DELHI BOMBAY CALCUTTA MADRAS KARACHI LAHORE DACCA
KUALA LUMPUR SINGAPORE HONG KONG TOKYO

ISBN 0 19 828195 1

© *Oxford University Press* 1974

*Printed in Great Britain
by William Clowes & Sons, Limited
London, Beccles and Colchester*

*To*
*Alexandros*

# Preface

It has been noted that developing countries with liberal policies towards foreign direct investments are not usually characterized by otherwise liberal regimes. Given the asymmetries that abound in political and economic relations the inverse is obviously not true.

This book attempts to examine some of the major economic reasons for controlling the activities of transnational enterprises in the Third World in so far as they affect the generation and distribution of income. The emphasis is mainly on two aspects of such firms: first, the effect on their conduct of oligopolistic market structures and the desire to foster their control over production and markets and over the public policies that they help to create and orient, and secondly, some of their structural characteristics, notably the degrees of integrated relations between affiliates, that help to explain their conduct. The enterprises examined operate across national boundaries but are not in any sense multinational, since key activities, such as the development of productive knowledge and the exercise of strategic managerial decision making, as well as their ownership and control, are concentrated in their home counties. Specific policies of the governments of such countries are devised to assist the enterprises in their world-wide operations. Yet the firms themselves do not always act in the interest of their country of origin, since their ultimate objective is corporate and not national.

A correct understanding of policies with regard to foreign direct investments and their effects needs to be incorporated within a political theory of the origin of such policies. The present book attempts to explore those elements of knowledge about the effects of the firms concerned on intercountry income distribution that help to explain how government policies are or should be worked out in host countries. Such knowledge, together with a specific political commitment and orientation, led the member nations of the Andean Pact in December 1970 to adopt a common policy towards foreign investments.

My debt to others in preparing this book is such that I cannot by any means express adequately the appreciation felt and the acknowledgements deserved. Only a few will be mentioned here. In particular I wish to thank the Junta del Acuerdo de Cartagena for giving me the opportunity to discuss my ideas and research with its members as well as with diverse government officials of the Andean Pact countries. The book is based on my Ph.D. dissertation presented at the Economics Department of Harvard University. During that period I profited especially from the advice of Albert O. Hirschman. Earlier shorter papers, that form part of the book, were considerably improved by comments from Paul Streeten, Raymond Vernon, Dwight Brothers, and members of the Harvard University Development Advisory Service. Most of my thanks, though, go to my colleagues in diverse government agencies in the Andean Pact, particularly the Planning Department of Colombia. Without their contribution and their willingness to share the time and data at their disposal, the work presented in this book would not have been possible.

*Lima, April 1974*                    CONSTANTINE V. VAITSOS

# Contents

# Introduction

THE literature on foreign direct investment can be separated into two broad areas of analysis, which undoubtedly have several interrelated parts. One area deals mostly with the *causes* that prompt the flow of capital together with other resources across national boundaries. It includes the traditional hypothesis (with limited empirical verification) of flows based on differentials of returns to capital among countries. More empirically significant hypotheses have been based, among other factors, on those that relate to monopoly positions through ownership of 'unique assets' by firms,[1] defensive strategies related to risk of loss of markets or of sources of supply,[2] changing technological ascendancy,[3] tariff levels,[4] product differentiation and seller's concentration,[5] organizational structures and strategies,[6] and others.[7] The second broad area of economic literature on foreign direct investments deals with the *effects* that such investments have, mostly, on the host countries.[8] The quantifiable effects basically relate to income

[1] This hypothesis was first adequately tested by Stephen H. Hymer in 'International Operations of National Firms: A Study of Direct Foreign Investment', unpublished Ph.D. dissertation, Massachusetts Institute of Technology, 1960.

[2] See, for example, Y. Aharoni, *The Foreign Investment Decision Process*, Harvard University Press, Cambridge, Mass., 1966.

[3] Referring to the risk of loss of export markets and the varying degrees of technological ascendancy over time are the studies related to the 'product cycle theory'. See for example R. Vernon, 'International Investment and International Trade in the Product Cycle', *Quarterly Journal of Economics*, vol. 80 (1966); L. Wells, Jr., 'Test of a Product Cycle Model of International Trade: U.S. Exports of Consumer Durables', *Quarterly Journal of Economics*, vol. 83 (1969); S. Hirsch, *Location of Industry and International Competitiveness*, Clarendon Press, Oxford, 1967.

[4] Thomas O. Horst, 'A Theoretical and Empirical Analysis of American Exports and Direct Investment', unpublished Ph.D. dissertation, University of Rochester, 1969.

[5] Richard E. Caves, 'International Corporations: The Industrial Economics of Foreign Investment', *Económica*, (Feb. 1971).

[6] For a survey and analysis see C. P. Kindleberger, *American Business Abroad*, Yale University Press, New Haven, Conn., 1969.

[7] For a collection of articles see C. P. Kindleberger, (ed.), *The International Corporation: A Symposium*, MIT Press, Cambridge, Mass., 1970.

[8] For examples of 'home' rather than 'host' country effects see C. G. Hufbauer and M. H. Adler, *Overseas Manufacturing Investment and the Balance of Payments*, U.S. Treasury Department, Washington, D.C., 1967.

and balance of payments measurements with qualitative state-ments on externalities.[9] It is of interest to observe that work using tools of welfare economics quite often concludes that, as far as non-quantifiable effects are concerned, the positive ones generally exceed the negative.[10] In contrast, several political scientists and political economists have noted that the negative non-quantifiable effects are far more important than the positive, equally non-quantifiable ones.[11] (Professional differences, repre-sented by the content even more than the methods of their analysis, often lead to diverging conclusions on the same subject.)

Most of the studies dealing with measurable variables can be characterized by their reference to a benefit–cost type of analysis related to *one* country, or *one* sector or project. The limitations of these quantitative approaches in taking into consideration the effects of foreign direct investments on some of the structural elements of the host countries, such as the impact on domestic entrepreneurial activities, have directed some economists to alternative formulations.[12] As far as developing countries are concerned these new formulations are gaining increasing validity in view of the dominant position of foreign corporations in the industrial base of the host countries and the high rate of acquisi-tions of local firms as a vehicle of entry by the foreign investors.[13]

Despite the diverse and very numerous analysis on the subject

[9] Several of the more sophisticated studies use, as a base, methodologies such as the one prepared by M. Bruno in *The Optimum Selection of Import Substitution and Export Promoting Projects*, United Nations, New York, 1964.

[10] See for example D. Schydlowsky, 'Benefit–Cost Analysis of Foreign Invest-ment Proposals', paper presented at the Dubrovnik Conference of Harvard Develop-ment Advisory, June 1970.

[11] See J. N. Behrman, 'Governmental Policy Alternative and the Problems of International Sharing', in J. H. Dunning (ed.), *The Multinational Enterprise*, George Allen & Unwin, London, 1971.

[12] See A. O. Hirschman, 'How to Divest in Latin America, and Why', *Essays in International Finance*, no. 76 (Princetown University, Nov., 1969). Also Celso Furtado, *Los Estados Unidos y del Subdesarrollo de América Latina*, Instituto de Estudios Peruanos, Lima, Apr. 1971. Work has been done on a broader framework by Osvaldo Sunkel in the Instituto de Estudios Internacionales, Santiago, Chile. For further references see Carlos F. Díaz Alejandro, 'Direct Foreign Investment in Latin America', in Kindleberger, op. cit., pp. 319–44; also F. Pazos, 'The Role of International Movements of Private Capital in Promoting Development', in *Capital Movements & Economic Development*, ed. S. H. Adler, Proceedings of a Confer-ence held by the International Economic Association, 1967.

[13] For figures of acquisitions of firms in Colombia and Peru by U.S. corporations see M. Wionczek, *Inversión y Tecnología Extranjera en América Latina*, Cuadernos de Joaquín Mortiz, México, 1971.

of foreign direct investment, not very much has been done on the distribution of its net effects between capital-exporting and 'host' countries.[14] No doubt the foreign investment model involves aspects related to a non-zero sum game: benefits can accrue to one of the participants which do not necessarily imply costs for the other. For example, the host country can obtain important spill-over effects through technical assistance, training and organizing of domestic suppliers, etc. The foreign investor can, in turn, obtain significant scale effects either in terms of risk diversification or in the 'spreading' of fixed overhead expenditures in production activities, R & D, etc. among various subsidiaries. Yet a very substantial part of the effects of foreign investment involves distributable elements. Furthermore, given the thesis presented later in this book, that foreign direct investments take place basically within a *bargaining framework*, both distributable *and* non-distributable elements enter in negotiations. This is so, since the sharing of the distributable elements can be conditioned on the non-distributable ones in a bargaining situation.

*behaviou ral*

As far as developing countries are concerned their industrial sectors are becoming increasingly controlled by the subsidiaries of foreign corporations whose local sales in many cases increase faster than those of nationally owned firms in the same or other sectors, or than the country's over-all economic activity.[15] (Gross estimates place the foreign control of the more dynamic Latin American sectors somewhere between 50 per cent and 75 per cent.) The distribution of the resulting income effects between host country and foreign investors is thus becoming an increasingly important part of the recipient's development strategy and achievement. Similarly, sales through the activities of subsidiaries in other countries are taking an increasing share in the global sales of transnational corporations. For example, from 1955 to 1964 the sales of manufacturing subsidiaries owned by U.S. transnational enterprises in the rest of the world increased by 170 per cent. The corresponding increase of sales of the same transnational corporations in their domestic market

---

[14] For an exception see H. W. Singer, 'The Distribution of Gains between Investing and Borrowing Countries', *American Economic Review* (May 1950). Also E. T. Penrose, 'Profit Sharing Between Producing Countries and Oil Companies in the Middle East', *Economic Journal*, vol. 69 (June 1959).

[15] See CORFO, *Comportamiento de las Principales Empresas Industriales Extranjeras Acogidas al D.F.L. 258*, Publication no. 9—A/70, Santiago, Chile.

was 50 per cent.[16] Thus, for both the capital-exporting and the capital-importing countries, income generated from activities of subsidiaries owned by the former in the markets of the latter constitute an increasingly significant economic factor. Evidence indicates that host government intervention in the receiving countries (both developed and developing) in their confrontation with foreign corporations is becoming a practice of increasing frequency. Projections estimate that such practices are likely to continue in the future.[17]

In the pages that follow we will deal with the reasons and mechanisms of intercountry income *distribution* resulting from interaffiliate charges in the operations of transnational corporations. In so doing, we will not analyse the relative income effects that stem from the overall economic strategy of nations related to the selection of certain economic activities where transnational enterprises could participate. Thus, we will not re-evaluate arguments on development based on primary activities versus those on industrialization. Nor will we deal with the income distribution effects implied by the selection of alterative techniques and technologies,[18] or by the selection of goods and services to be produced. (The latter selection is determined, among other factors, by the existing income distribution and, in turn, influences income distribution.) Rather, we will be concerned with the factors that have an effect on intercountry income distribution once the affiliates of transnational enterprises are established in the countries concerned, given sectors, activities, and production techniques.

Chapter I of the book discusses the proposition that foreign direct investment and/or technology commercialization take place in a package form where various factors of production and

---

[16] Data from various years published by the Survey of Current Business as analysed by Celso Furtado, op. cit., p. 33. For an analysis of the impact on the structure of foreign investments resulting from different market growth rates see S. Hymer and R. Rowthorn, 'Multinational Corporations and International Oligopoly: The Non-American Challenge', in C. Kindleberger (ed.), pp. 57–91.

[17] See R. Vernon, 'Future of the Multinational Enterprise' in C. Kindleberger, (ed.), pp. 373–400.

[18] See A. K. Sen, *Choice of Technique*, Blackwell, Oxford, 1960; also W. Galenson and H. Leitenstein, 'Investment Criteria, Productivity and Economic Development', *Quarterly Journal of Economics* (Aug. 1955); and Francis Stewart, 'Choice of Techniques in Developing Countries', mim., Queen Elizabeth House, Oxford, Oct. 1970.

other inputs are collectively involved. Since inputs are transferred collectively, their returns have also to be evaluated in a collective form. Interdependence among inputs exists both with respect to the causal factors that prompt their use as well as with respect to the returns that jointly accrue to them. Furthermore, the chapter discusses the mechanisms by which such collective resource flows enable the supplier partly or totally to preserve certain monopoly positions and monopoly rents, at least during certain periods of time, and thus countervail opposing competitive forces.

Chapter II presents a critical review of the theory on inter-country income distribution that results from increased factor availability as well as from the inflow (outflow) of factors of production across national boundaries. Furthermore, it describes the interdependence that exists between intra- and inter-country income effects for both host and factor-exporting economies. Finally reference is made to the inapplicability of the assumptions and conclusions of the capital flows theory in the foreign direct investment model. In the presence of transnational enterprises, foreign direct investment is best understood within an oligopoly model involving collective factor or resource transfers, where capital is probably assuming a decreasing importance. Within such a market structure and performance related to global strate-gies by firms, adequate analysis requires tools that belong more to the theory of industrial organizations rather than to inter-national capital movements.

In introducing the empirical evidence, Chapter III presents the methodology undertaken for the data collection of the research, sample definition, and industries studied in the countries of the Andean Pact. It also describes the sources of information used and the mechanism of data analysis. Chapter IV presents the empirical findings of the research. It first analyses data related to the importance of the joint sale of intermediate products and capital goods within the foreign direct investment and/or technology commercialization models. The overpricing of imports traded among affiliates proved to be a common practice in all four industries studied in Colombia and in two industries in Chile, Ecuador, and Peru, where comparatively smaller samples were undertaken. The implicit returns accruing through such product overpricing appeared, in several cases, far to outweigh the explicit returns to factors of production. In addition, this chapter analyses data on export prohibitive clauses and other restrictive business practices exercised through contracts of technology commercialization. Finally, some of the implications on measurements of value added, effective profitability, and comparative gains between host countries and foreign investors are analysed as a result of the accrual of factor returns through the pricing of products tied to them.

An interpretation of the empirical results is undertaken in Chapter V. This includes an evaluation of the effects that foreign investments had on limiting external and internal competitive pressures in the Colombian manufacturing sector within the import substitution strategy pursued by that country in the late 1960s. The effective profitability accruing to the foreign investors was determined, to a great extent, by these market conditions. The second section of the chapter analyses the different channels of remission of their effective profitability that were preferred by foreign investors in view of specific host government policies and their own business strategy. Specific differences were noted and analysed between industries due to their different characteristics and state of development in the Colombian economy. Also, differences in results between firms were analysed in view of diverging ownership structures. Finally, different policies pursued by the governments of the Andean Pact countries in the late 1960s were used as an explanatory variable in comparing differences in behaviour by foreign investors.

Chapter VI presents a conceptual analysis of the factors that effect the preferences of transnational corporations as to which country or countries they select for declaration of income from their global activities with corresponding intercountry income distribution implications. In the presence of neutral government policies (e.g. zero-profit tax *differentials* among countries and zero costs on transfer pricing) three factors were analysed which explained company preferences as to the location of income declaration. One referred to the comparison between the costs incurred by an affiliate for the global operations of a transnational enterprise, present and future, and its earnings from sales in its domestic market and to non-affiliates abroad. The second referred to differences in the opportunity cost of company-generated funds among countries during different time periods. The third referred to over-all business tactics related to (a) transfer pricing and the revenues of the *paying* affiliates, (b) pricing policies and technological ascendancy in various productive stages of vertically integrated firms, (c) interaffiliate charges and some political considerations, and (d) interaffiliate debt–equity structures. In the latter part of the chapter we study the effects on company behaviour (with respect to interaffiliate charges) that result from specific government policies. The latter include (a) differentials among countries on corporate taxes, (b) indirect fiscal charges affecting transfer pricing, (c) requirements for local participation in the ownership of firms, and (d) limits or negotiable levels on profit and royalty remissions.

Chapter VII evaluates the foreign investment model within a bargaining framework as an alternative to analyses based on partial benefit/cost estimates. Different negotiable elements are noted as well as different forms of exercise of bargaining power among host countries and foreign investors. Also, the first section of the chapter explains part of the *a priori* indeterminancy of outcomes within the foreign investment model evaluated in a bargaining framework. The second section presents empirical analysis on the negotiating results of the Colombian Comité de Regalías (Committee of Royalties) in the 1967–70 period as well as a brief evaluation of some of its weaknesses in bargaining. The final section of the chapter compares parallel situations in the experience of developing countries between their negotiations in extractive industries, during the first part of this century, and their bargaining performance in technology licensing agreements in the manufacturing sector during the last two decades.

# CHAPTER I

# Collective Inputs and Monopoly

TRADITIONAL economic theory has greatly conditioned its pupils to think of the case of capital flows among countries as the transfer of a single factor of production which is missing in the recipient's country and which complements the existing factors. Statements like the following, in the neo-classical tradition of international trade, abound in economic literature: 'Capital flows from relatively capital-rich to capital-poor countries tend to equalize "factor proportions" in both countries and thus to reduce the basis for commodity trade.'[1] Similarly, economists (treating technology basically as an aggregate entity which, introduced as an index in the production function, augments the availability of some or all of the other inputs in terms of efficiency units[2]) generally evaluate technology and its absorption in the form of a single factor flow.

The analysis presented in this book refers to the proposition that resource flows (whether capital or technology or both) take place in a package form where, in most cases, more than one factor of production is involved.

The effects that this package has on economic performance or behaviour portray an interdependence in the structural relationship that exists between the components that comprise the collective unit. We will argue that such an interdependence implies a two-way directional causality between any two of the individual elements or a multi-directional causality among a larger number of them. For example, the flow of direct investment by a particular capital supplier (as distinct from portfolio investments) will tend to affect the type of technology concomitantly forthcoming and, in various ways, the managerial strategy and performance or the administrative practices exercised. Similarly,

---

[1] P. B. Musgrave, *United States Taxation of Foreign Investment Income, Issues and Arguments*, Harvard Law School, Cambridge, Mass., 1969, p. 22.

[2] For a survey of the literature see F. H. Hahn and R. C. O. Mathews, 'The Theory of Economic Growth—A Survey', *Economic Journal* (1964), part II.

the managerial know-how used could affect the size and composition of capital through such elements as the debt–equity ratio of the recipient or the relationship between equity and loans by the parent to the subsidiary. Also, the technology supplied will tend to affect the size and type of capital goods and intermediate products that the affiliated firm imports from its parent. In turn, such imports could affect the size of the direct investment as well as of any interaffiliate loans needed to finance part of the fixed and current assets of the recipient.

Since inputs are introduced jointly in the production function of a firm, returns accrue collectively to the supplier of the package of resources. The price registered for the collective input will, in addition to directly identifiable costs of some of its components (e.g. the price of natural rubber going into the manufacture of tires), reflect the allocation of overheads among countries (e.g. R & D expenses undertaken in country $x$ and shared through royalty payments by countries $x, y$, and $z$ where affiliates operate) and/or the allocation of overheads among products involved in a joint production (e.g. the expenses for designing, tooling, testing, etc. a car are shared among the components of a kit exported for assembly abroad). Furthermore, the price of the collective input will also reflect the rents accruing to it as a result of market conditions.

To the extent that, in certain industries, overheads undertaken for the global operations and allocated intercountry- and/or interproduct-wise, and also to the extent that the accrual of rents from certain markets become a substantial part of the total sales of an affiliate in a country, the price paid for a collective unit could greatly depend on the relative bargaining power among the participating parties (e.g. the host country and the foreign investors). Such bargaining could be exercised indirectly through, for example, the setting of tariffs which protect or, in the case of importers, create additional costs. Or it could be exercised directly in actual negotiating situations on royalty payments, subsidies, etc. Furthermore, the price declared for each one of the components of the collective input can only be understood if the simultaneous relationships between such components are reduced to an understanding of the factors that affect them, such as home and host government policies, industry and/or market structures, and finally the business strategy of the participating firms. These issues will be explored in later chapters.

In addition, the collective flow of resources and products within the foreign investment model creates in itself (partially as a result of the transferrer's motives and partially as a result of conditions describing the recipient host country and its entrepreneurs) the seeds of monopoly power. The supplier can attempt to maintain such a power during different time periods by arranging product or collective resource flows in such a manner as to counteract the competitive pressure that might arise during the economic life of a particular activity. The effective maintenance of monopoly power by controlling the process of resource flows can result in outcomes of production, or efficiency, or distribution of benefits that far outweigh the results of traditionally defined analysis of factors of production. Foreign direct investment in developing countries, because of the influence of this element of monopoly power, has the '. . . very high degree of ambiguity of most human inventions and institutions: it has considerable potential for both good and evil'.[3]

Relatively recent theoretical and empirical work has led to the development of a new formulation that attempts to explain the forces that generate commodity, service, and factor flows among nations.[4] This formulation is referred to in the literature as the product cycle theory.[4a] According to it, when a new product or

[3] A. O. Hirschman, 'How to Divest in Latin America, and Why', p. 3.

[4] Gordon K. Douglas, 'Product Variation and International Trade in Motion Pictures', unpublished Ph.D. dissertation, Department of Economics, MIT, Cambridge, Mass., 1963. Seev Hirsch, *Location of Industry and International Competitiveness*, Clarendon Press, Oxford, 1967. Gary C. Hufbauer, *Synthetic Materials and the Theory of International Trade*, Harvard University Press, Cambridge, Mass., 1966. Donald Keesing, 'Labor Skills and Comparative Advantages', *American Economic Review*, vol. 56, no. 2 (May 1966), pp. 249–58. S. G. Moussouris, 'Export Horizons of Greek Industry', unpublished doctoral dissertation, Harvard Business School, Boston, Mass., 1968. Robert B. Stoubaugh, Jr., 'The Product Life Cycle, U.S. Exports, and International Investment', unpublished doctoral dissertation, Harvard Business School, Boston, Mass., 1968. Yoshihiro Tsurumi, 'Technology Transfer and Foreign Trade: The Case of Japan, 1950–1966', unpublished doctoral dissertation, Harvard Business School, Boston, Mass., 1968. William Gruber, Dileep Mehta, and Raymond Vernon, 'The R & D Factor in International Trade and International Investment of United States Industry', *Journal of Political Economy* (Fall, 1966). Raymond Vernon, 'International Investment and International Trade in the Product Cycle', *Quarterly Journal of Economics*, vol. 80 (May 1966), pp. 190–207. Louis T. Wells, Jr., 'Test of a Product Cycle Model of International Trade: U.S. Exports of Consumer Durables', *Quarterly Journal of Economics* (Feb. 1969).

[4a] In the latter part of the 1960s a new phenomenon began to be felt, in the process of international investment and international trade, of particular interest to developing countries. Vertically integrated transnational enterprises intensified

process is first developed, the technology related to it is usually maintained by the few firms which originated it or which could copy it from the leaders. Legal 'captivity' (i.e. patents) or strictly technical 'captivity' (generated through experimentation, experi- X ence with the design, etc.) render the market heavily monopolistic. In addition, due to the novelty of the product, its 'highly differentiated nature . . . and the characteristics of the customers who buy new products [mostly high income consumers][5] . . . all result in a low price-elasticity of demand both for the product as a whole and for the individual firm.'[6] Thus, during the early stages of a 'product cycle' the innovators and their initial imitators operate within a market that (a) by the nature of the product has an inelastic demand and (b) by the nature of the stage (an early one) has very few competitors. These market qualities and structure enable the first comers to enjoy monopoly positions, which help to compensate for part or all of the expenses of R & D, the risk of launching into new areas, etc. In addition, when products flow across national boundaries during these early stages, they are in the form of final goods until minimum size and cost considerations as well as competitive pressures force the building of a new plant 'abroad'. In subsequent stages of the 'product cycle', when technology and tastes are standardized, the original producers and their first imitators, in response to the risk of loss of final product markets, as a defensive strategy,[7] move into direct investments in subsidiaries, or joint ventures or perhaps, into licensing agreements. In the final product markets a specific threat is faced which in turn is created by able, new imitators as well as by barriers set up by governments pursuing

their world-wide sourcing of cheap inputs, locating part of their production activities in areas where the costs of local factors of production were (significantly) lower than in other parts of their world-wide activities. With respect to international investment theory this phenomenon seriously questions models that interpret the international location of production of transnational firms on the basis of different stages over time, like the product cycle theory. See G. H. Heileiner, 'Manufactured Exports from Less-Developed Countries and Multinational Firms', *Economic Journal* (Mar. 1973), pp. 21–47, and G. Adám, 'New Trends in International Business: World Wide Sourcing and Dedomiciling', *Acta Oeconomica*, vol. 7, nos. 3–4 (1971), pp. 349–69.

[5] For an early treatment of this aspect see S. Burenstam-Linder, *An Essay on Trade and Transformation*, Almqvist and Wiksell, Stockholm, 1961.

[6] L. Wells, Jr., 'Vehicles for the International Transfer of Technology', Teknoloji Ve Iktisadi Kalkvuma, [conference at] Istanbul, 1969, p. 5.

[7] See Y. Aharoni, *The Foreign Investment Decision Process*, Harvard University Press, Cambridge, Mass., 1967.

import substitution policies. During these later stages the exporter moves from the sale of final goods to that of primary inputs (capital, technology) and of intermediate products (provided that the economics of the industry permit it).

Although the 'product cycle' theorists have quite extensively examined these stages, they have not, we feel, adequately treated a key element in the whole transfer mechanism, namely the monopoly powers as they are enjoyed during the different stages involved. As was stated above, monopolistic positions are achieved as a result of innovations or technically advanced processes in the early stages of the life cycle of a product. This can be called a 'technological monopoly'. The returns generated by such monopoly positions set into motion opposing competitive forces by the inducement that such returns have for potential new entrants by imitation. These monopoly-diluting forces will tend to depend on various factors. Some obvious ones will appear to be, first, the size itself of potential returns that newcomers foresee in copying the original innovators, and, second, the degree of complexity that new processes or products imply for such imitators. Given the size of monopoly returns and the complexity of technology, some additional economic elements will tend to affect the degree of monopoly dilution. One of them will be related to the existing structure (with respect to already functioning firms) and the sophistication of the industry where an innovation takes place. For example, the textiles industry portrays a structure with relatively no major international technological differences within each family of textile products. Furthermore, a considerable number of different textile firms exist in the world. Thus, new technological processes or products in this industry are likely to be incorporated by more producers and more quickly than in, let us say, the electronics computer industry. Thus, technological monopoly positions are likely to be diluted much faster in the former industry by existing firms. Additional elements involve the over-all business orientation and propensities of the business community to translate scientific and technological inventions into commerciable process and product innovations.[8] Similarly, the extent of skill diversification and specialization which makes possible the absorption and use of

[8] For industry analyses on this point see studies by OECD on *Gaps in Technology*, Paris, 1968.

knowledge in an industry and/or country will also affect the degree of successful imitation by latecomers.[9]

These and other elements will determine the extent of maintenance of technology-induced monopoly power. The resulting countervailing forces could be quite strong. For example, a study undertaken in the petrochemicals industry indicated that, in the time period during which technology was sold to developing countries, in the life cycle of certain products, the original producers accounted for only 1 per cent of the total licensing. The remaining 99 per cent was divided between followers of commercial producers (52 per cent) and engineering firms (47 per cent).[10]

What is the role, then, of the transnational corporation *in its foreign direct investment undertaking* with respect to these monopoly-diluting forces? Does it accentuate them or does it retard them or even block them? How is concentration of production, or more important, of sales, in countries (particularly in developing ones) explained in the presence of diluting factors in technologically originated monopoly? Contrast the figures presented above on petrochemicals with the industry concentration (which includes various sectors) in a country like Chile. In the latter country, in a sample taken of foreign-owned manufacturing subsidiaries, 50 per cent had a monopoly or duopoly position in the host market. Another 36·4 per cent were operating in an oligopoly market where they had a leader's position. Only 13·6 per cent of the foreign subsidiaries in the sample controlled less than 25 per cent of the local market.[11]

If transnational corporations enter a new market with new products via the foreign investment road rather than through exportation, such expansive activities increase competitive forces, at least for a certain period, as a direct result of the investment process. However, the product cycle theory teaches us that foreign investments, to a large extent, are undertaken as a defensive strategy to maintain *already* established market positions and

---

[9] See Celso Furtado, *Development & Underdevelopment*, University of California Press, Berkeley, Calif., 1964.

[10] See R. Stobaugh, 'Utilizing Technical Know-how in a Foreign Investment and Licensing Program', paper presented in the National Meeting, Chemical Marketing Research Association, New York City, Feb. 1970, p. 5.

[11] See CORFO, *Comportamiento de las Principales Empresas Industriales Extranjeras Acogidas al D. F. L. 258*, Publicación no. 9-A/70, Santiago, Chile, p. 16.

to prevent potential competitors from displacing the original exporters or licensors. In that sense, the process of foreign investment retards competitive forces and is directed towards the preservation of (monopoly) positions.

Studies on the monopoly or oligopoly-inducing effects resulting from the foreign direct investment process[12] have singled out various factors that result in such market effects. Some of them refer to size of firms,[13] others to technological and managerial capacities and requirements,[14] still others to acquisition and merger processes.[15]

In this book we will deal with the effects on monopoly preservation that result from the collective resource and product flows within the foreign investment model. Such input collectivity might imply the creation of monopoly power both within and between inputs where, otherwise, competitive conditions could have existed. The case of monopoly creation within categories of inputs can be seen from the following. The sale and use of advanced technology can be tied to that of a much earlier vintage for which competitors are available. For example, several anti-trust suits have been brought against the International Business Machine Co. by its North American competitors for tying the sale of its software to that of hardware. Competition exists for the latter, yet it is limited or excluded by tying its usage with the former where a technological ascendancy exists.

The history of foreign direct investment often portrays or has

---

[12] See S. Hymer's Ph.D. dissertation, and 'Direct Foreign Investment and National Interest', in *Nationalism in Canada*, ed. P. Russel, McGraw-Hill, Toronto, 1966; 'Anti-Trust and American Direct Investment Abroad', *International Aspects of Anti-Trust*, Hearings before the Subcommittee on Anti-trust and Monopoly of the Committee of the Judiciary, United States Senate, 89th Congress, Second Session, U.S. Government Printing Office, Washington, D.C., 1967.

[13] For example, in 1957, 15 out of 1,542 U.S. firms controlled 35% of total American manufacturing investments abroad while 1,463 firms, at the other end, shared 31% of the total. See U.S. Department of Commerce, 'U.S. Business Investments in Foreign Countries', Washington, D.C., 1960. For the U.K., 46 firms controlled 71% of manufacturing assets abroad and 3 firms had practically all foreign assets in the petroleum industry abroad. See W. B. Reddaway, *Effects of U.K. Direct Investment Overseas*, Cambridge University Press, Cambridge, 1967.

[14] J.-J. Servan-Schreiber, *Le Défi americain*, Édition de Noel, Paris, 1967; C. Layton, *Trans-Atlantic Investments*, The Atlantic Institute, Boulogne-sur-Seine, 1966. At the national level see J. K. Galbraith, *The New Industrial State*, Houghton Mifflin Company, Boston, Mass., 1967.

[15] S. Hymer and R. Rowthorn, 'Multinational Corporation and International Oligopoly: The Non-American Challenge', in C. Kindleberger (ed.), p. 85.

been the result of such packaged input sales. For example, Argentina was capable in the 1960s of using on her own or buying from independent suppliers the know-how employed in drilling for petroleum. Yet the technology embodied in equipment for such activities was controlled by a few firms which tied its availability to the actual extractive operations through foreign direct investment.

Such tie-in arrangements do not only stem from the supplier's motives but also from the conditions that characterize recipients. Bringing together various inputs involved in a project, such as the plant design necessary to apply specific process technologies, requires special knowledge and skills which the buyer might not have. He prefers then to buy them collectively from one source although various individual input technologies might exist.[16] Thus, whether as a result of suppliers' motives or conditions characterizing recipients, the collective sale of inputs prolongs market concentration in a process of sequential monopoly adjustments and hence limits potential competitive forces.

Similarly, package resource flows between categories of inputs have equivalent effects of monopoly preservation. Even if local entrepreneurs in a country could have access to different sources of know-how in the petrochemical industry, the high capital requirements for investment might necessitate the tied purchase of know-how from firms which have the funds to provide for the investments needed. Such a case was noted in the British tobacco industry in the beginning of the century where the coexistence of marketing know-how and large sums of money to apply it by the American Tobacco Company reduced, through the process of foreign direct investment, a market where more than thirteen firms had originally competed to a duopoly situation. Finally, through market sharing, complete monopoly in individual markets was achieved.[17] Or patent holders could extend their legally granted privileges into other areas like the concomitant sale of products and capital.

A certain degree of competition could exist between firms that

[16] This applies particularly to developing countries. See Charles Cooper, 'Transfer of Technology from Advanced to Developing Countries', study prepared for the Secretariats of ACAST and UNCTAD, Nov. 1970.

[17] See J. H. Dunning, *American Investment in British Manufacturing Industry*, George Allen & Unwin Ltd., London, 1958, pp. 30–1.

can combine all elements of the package of resources necessary. Yet the presence itself of collective inputs limits or excludes potential competitors for each one of the individual elements and hence reduces the number of potential competitors to, possibly, an oligopoly market. This, in turn, could result in such an interdependence among potential competitors, in their market shares, that explicit or implicit collusion or accommodations might be sought.[18] An example of this can be seen in the present cartelization of the South American electronics industry, with a strong hold in Argentina by Siemens, in Brazil by North American firms, and in part of the Andean market by Philips International. In some industries, such as textiles, long processes of competitive forces and special sector characteristics, such as raw materials availability, have 'opened up' the package of inputs in such a way as to limit monopoly positions. It is precisely in such industries that transnational enterprises undertake disinvestments on their own initiative. For example, as part of company strategy, because of limited monopoly position and relatively restricted demand potentials, Grace Co. is divesting itself of its role in the Latin American textiles sector and moving into pulp and paper (where it controls technology in the use of sugar cane as input) and into certain chemicals.

Finally, we will simply mention another element, to be treated more extensively in later chapters, which refers to the monopoly-inducing effects of foreign direct investments resulting from their impact on the execution of import-substituting strategies of host countries, particularly the developing ones. The collective flow of foreign inputs accompanying foreign investment and the pricing of such inputs often affect the type of tariff and non-tariff protection offered to them.

Thus, potentially competitive import markets are replaced by highly monopolistic input and output ones partly as a result of the conditions on entry presented by the foreign investors. The case of Chile will again serve as an example. A high concentration in the total payments made to transnational enterprises, by sector, with respect to the country of destination of such payments, was noted for the late 1960s. Chilean licensees (national and foreign-owned), with 399 contracts analysed, paid for royalties, profit remissions, intermediates, etc. the following percentages

18 See S. Hymer and R. Rowthorn, op. cit., pp. 57–94.

of the total outlays by sector to the various countries shown in Table I.1.

TABLE I.1

| Sector | Countries | Percentage of total payments by the whole sector going to the countries that appear in the previous column % |
|---|---|---|
| Food and beverages | Switzerland and U.S.A. | 96·6 |
| Tobacco | United Kingdom | 100·0 |
| Industrial chemicals | W. Germany and Switzerland | 96·6 |
| Other chemicals | U.S.A., W. Germany and Switzerland | 92·0 |
| Petroleum and coal products | U.S.A. and United Kingdom | 100·0 |
| Rubber products | U.S.A. | 99·9 |
| Non-metalic minerals | U.S.A. | 97·0 |
| Metallic products (except equipment) | U.S.A. | 94·0 |
| Non-electric machinery | U.S.A. | 98·7 |
| Electric equipment | Holland, U.S.A., Spain | 92·0 |
| Transport equipment | France, Switzerland | 89·0 |

SOURCE: G. Oxman, 'La Balanza de Pagos Tecnológicos de Chile', mim., Sept. 1971.

Obviously, the type of technology imported by Chile implies, even at the country level, a much broader availability of sources of supply of equipment, intermediates, capital, etc., than Table I.1 indicates. Yet the acceptance of a particular foreign investor, contractually or otherwise, might exclude the possibility of tapping alternative sources of supply. Furthermore, individual firm analysis, to be presented later in this book, indicated that the concentration indices in Table I.1 reflected in practice individual firms involved which tied the importation of technology, direct capital, debt, intermediates, equipment, etc., to the same source of supply.

Hence the fruits of monopoly in final product markets, enjoyed in the early stages of the product cycle due to technological ascendancy, can be partially or totally preserved in later periods by the institutional mechanisms of collective product and factor flows in the foreign direct investment model. Thus, a technological monopoly is transformed into an *institutional* one. *Viewed in this light the product cycle theory is seen as a theory of monopoly cycles.*

# CHAPTER II

# Factor Flows and Income Distribution[1]

## A. INCREASED FACTOR AVAILABILITY AND INTERCOUNTRY INCOME DISTRIBUTION

Given certain critical underlying assumptions, standard growth theory suggests the following, about the effects of increased factor availability on trade[2] and this, in turn, on real income. Technical progress will tend to improve a country's terms of trade if such progress is introduced in the import sector, and worsen them if introduced in the export industry.[3] Similarly, enhanced capital utilization will improve a country's terms of trade if its imports are relatively capital intensive, and worsen them if its exports are relatively capital intensive.[4] In both cases intercountry income distribution (expressed by real income measurements) takes place through the price effects of expansion and trade. The output effects (related to the price ones) will depend, in addition, on the availability of other units of factors of production which, in combination with the additional capital or technology units, increase production. Thus full employment assumptions and displacement of any existing economic activities[5]

---

[1] This chapter appeared as part of a paper by C. V. Vaitsos on 'Intercountry Income Distribution, Welfare Considerations and Transnational Enterprises', to appear in J. H. Dunning (ed.), *Economic Analysis and the Multinational Enterprise*, Allen and Unwin, forthcoming.

[2] See J. R. Hicks, 'An Inaugural Lecture', *Oxford Economic Papers*, N.S. vol. 5, no. 2 (June 1953), and W. M. Corden, 'Economic Expansion and International Trade: A Geometric Approach', *ibid.*, N.S. vol. 8, no. 2 (June 1956).

[3] For example, see H. G. Johnson, 'Economic Expansion and International Trade', *The Manchester School of Economic and Social Studies*, vol. 23, no. 2 (May 1955), pp. 95–112. Also see R. Findlay and H. Grubert, 'Factor Intensity, Technological Progress, and the Terms of Trade', *Oxford Economic Papers*, N.S. vol. 11, no. 1, (Feb. 1959), pp. 111–21.

[4] See H. G. Johnson, 'The Efficiency and Welfare Implications of the International Corporation', in C. P. Kindleberger (ed.), *The International Corporation*, MIT Press, Cambridge, Mass., 1970, p. 43.

[5] This point is related to the acquisition of local firms by foreign enterprises as a vehicle of entry in the foreign direct investment model.

are critical in the measurement of the additional real income created.

The interdependence between increased economic activity and external trade can, under certain conditions, lead to a deterioration of the real income of the output-expanding economy with corresponding intercountry income distribution effects. This can occur if the increased supply of goods creates such a deterioration to the terms of trade of the expanding country that the gains from the increased output are more than offset by the relative price changes. Such an outcome leads to 'immiserizing growth'.[6]

There are two more examples of 'immiserizing growth' that need to be mentioned, which have particular relevance in the case of foreign direct investments. Both of them refer to the manner by which additional factors of production are allocated. Each one of them has varying degrees of effects on intercountry income distribution. The first case refers to the misallocation of additional factors of production in the presence of tariffs.[7] More of misallocated factors of production can result in net welfare losses rather than to additional welfare even if such factors are domestically owned.[8] If such factors of production are foreign-owned, then returns paid to them further reduce the welfare of the factor-receiving country through intercountry income flows.[9] A second form of 'immiserizing growth' can occur in cases of monopoly in product or factor markets where spatial discriminatory policies could result in similar income-generating and income distribution effects as the ones mentioned above with respect to tariffs.[10]

Simple, first-best arguments in the above two cases will suggest

[6] See J. Bhagwati, 'Immiserizing Growth: A Geometrical Note', *Review of Economic Studies*, vol. 25, no. 3, (June 1958), pp. 201–5.

[7] See H. G. Johnson, 'The Possibility of Income Losses from Increased Efficiency or Factor Accumulation in the Presence of Tariffs', *Economic Journal*, vol. 77, no. 305 (Mar. 1967), pp. 151–4.

[8] See Carlos F. Díaz Alejandro, 'Direct Foreign Investment in Latin America', in C. P. Kindleberger (ed.), pp. 325–6.

[9] For a numerical example see P. Streeten, 'Costs and Benefits of Multinational Enterprises in Less-Developed Countries', in J. H. Dunning (ed.), *The Multinational Enterprise*.

[10] 'If the direct investor can take over a competitor, perhaps the only competitor in a national market, he can establish a monopoly which may prove costly for the economy', see C. P. Kindleberger, 'Restrictions on Direct Investments in Host Countries', a discussion paper for the University of Chicago Workshop on International Business (5 Mar., 1969, unpublished), p. 9.

policies that should correct the corresponding market mal-functioning (e.g. reduce tariffs and introduce anti-trust or anti-monopoly policies). Yet, as will be discussed in later pages, the existence of tariffs is not independent of the particular forms in which certain factors of production are made available (for example, foreign direct investments especially in developing countries). Similarly, particular monopoly situations arise as a direct result of the form in which additional factors of production are transferred intercountry-wise. Experience has shown that, quite often, anti-monopoly policies have either partial effects or they lead to additional policy-induced distortions. Thus, they could constitute lesser best solutions.[11]

Summarizing the above, we can conclude that, under competitive market conditions, intercountry income distribution effects that accrue due to increased factor availability are a result of relative price changes. Additional considerations are involved in the presence of tariffs, the existence of monopoly conditions or the foreign origin of the additional factor availability. We pass now to discussing the effects of the latter case.

## B. FOREIGN FACTOR FLOWS AND INTERCOUNTRY INCOME DISTRIBUTION

If increased factor availability has a foreign origin then the above conclusions on intercountry income distribution need to be further qualified by the effects of payments to foreign factors of production. In terms of welfare considerations a distinction needs to be made between capital and already developed technology due to the public good character of the latter. In such a case payments are made for a non-exhaustible factor of production.

Under perfect market conditions and in the absence of tariffs the effects of payments to foreign factors of production can only be part or all of the income generated from the use of such foreign inputs in the host country.[12] The latter could be sharing

---

[11] For empirical examples where the combination of protection from foreign competition and domestic monopoly situations lead to income losses in the Colombian pharmaceutical industry where foreign investors control most of the local market, see C. V. Vaitsos, 'Transfer of Resources and Preservation of Monopoly Rents', Economic Development Report no. 168, Center of International Affairs, Harvard University, Cambridge, Mass., 1970, p. 64.

[12] Edith Tilton Penrose, 'Foreign Investment and the Growth of the Firm', Economic Journal, vol. 66 (June 1956), pp. 220–35.

some of the benefits in the form of higher returns to domestic factors of production and/or higher tax earnings of the host government and/or lower prices for the local consumer[13] and/or non-remitted profits by foreign investors leading to net capital formation. In the presence, though, of tariffs, or under imperfect market conditions, payments to foreign factors of production will accentuate the conclusions reached above on 'immiserizing growth'. Returns to foreign factors could, in such cases, exceed host country gains leading to net negative (income) effects.

In the case of foreign capital inflows there are two terms of trade that affect intercountry income distribution. (Parallel analysis can be undertaken in the case of technology inflows.) The first refers to the traditionally defined commodity terms of trade that relate to the relative prices of the traded goods as affected by capital flows. The second refers to the real value of the payments (receipts) for receiving (exporting) capital. Call it terms of borrowing. The joint effect of these two terms of trade, given prevailing market and production conditions, will determine the net effect on a country's real income resulting from capital inflows. It will also determine the relative distribution of benefits resulting from such investment activities. Furthermore, the two terms of trade are interdependent through technology, tariffs, transportation costs, etc.

As long as these two terms of trade move both in the same direction with respect to a country's gain (or loss), then the corresponding conclusions are obvious. If on the other hand the two terms of trade move in opposite directions then the net result will depend on the following two factors: (a) the degree of capital or labour intensity of the country's production function for the goods produced (forgone) due to the inflow (outflow) of foreign (national) capital; and (b) the relative importance of the goods concerned in the total basket of goods and services produced and traded. Take, for example, the case of first-best policy considerations on optimum tariff level. Under incomplete specialization, if a country is capital-importing and commodity-import substituting, the existence and level of optimum tariff will depend on the effect that such a tariff will have on improving commodity terms of trade, on worsening terms of borrowing, the

[13] See H. G. Johnson, 'The Efficiency and Welfare Implications of the International Corporation', p. 45.

degree of capital intensity of goods produced through the foreign factor inflows under tariff protection, and their relative importance on commodity trade.[14]

The way benefits, accruing to a country from trade, can be enhanced through unilateral restrictions (or inducements) has long been treated in the relevant literature on tariffs. Similar arguments have evolved in the case of capital flows both for borrowing and lending countries.[15] If the services of capital are considered as a traded good then interference in its flow can be incorporated in the over-all analysis of the optimum tariff concept for maximizing national gains. This is particularly true if the services of capital are considered as a consumption good, a usual simplification in growth theory.[16] Additional considerations, though, arise in cases where the services of capital are considered as an intermediate rather than as a consumption good. Optimal effective tax (or subsidy) rules on capital flows have been estimated in the case of different consumer valuations of traded goods in two countries.[17]

The optimum capital tax rate depends not only on technology (which specifies the relative factor intensity of goods produced

[14] For a description of the symmetrical results due to differing capital intensity of traded goods among capital exporting and importing countries in the presence of tariff policies see R. W. Jones, 'International Capital Movements and the Theory of Tariffs and Trade', *Quarterly Journal of Economics*, vol. 81, no. 1 (Feb. 1967), pp. 10–11.

[15] See M. C. Kemp, 'Foreign Investment and the National Advantage', *Economic Record*, vol. 38 (Mar. 1962); id., 'The Benefits and Costs of Private Investment from Abroad: Comment', *Economic Record*, vol. 38 (Mar. 1962); id., 'The Gain from International Trade and Investment: A Neo-Heckscher-Ohlin Approach', *American Economic Review*, vol. 56 (Sept. 1966). Also see G. D. A. MacDougall, 'The Benefits and Costs of Private Investment from Abroad: A Theoretical Approach', *Economic Record*, vol. 36 (Mar. 1960), and T. Balogh and P. Streeten, 'Domestic versus Foreign Investment', *Bulletin of the Oxford University Institute of Statistics*, vol. 22 (Aug. 1960). For earlier treatments see Carl Iversen, *Aspects of the Theory of International Capital Movements*, London, 1936, pp. 160–70. Also J. M. Keynes, 'Foreign Investment and National Advantage', *The Nation and Atheneum*, 9 Aug. 1924, pp. 584–7, and *A Treatise on Money*, vol. 1, Macmillan, London, 1930, pp. 343–6. Also A. K. Cairncross, 'Home and Foreign Investment 1807–1913', *Review of Economic Studies* (Oct. 1935), pp. 67–78.

[16] For example, in the case of three consumption goods, two commodities, and the services of capital, it would pay to subsidize trade in one of them. See J. de V. Graaff, *Theoretical Welfare Economics*, Cambridge University Press, Cambridge, 1957, pp. 136–7.

[17] Such differences in valuations are expressed by differences in market prices, maintained through tariffs on imports or subsidies on exports. See R. W. Jones, pp. 12–14.

and traded), but also on the elasticity of foreign import demand. The value of the latter depends on the price level at which it is being calculated, which in turn depends on the choice of the objective function chosen for maximization. Thus, as in the case of optimal tariff, the optimal tax rate on capital flows is not unique.[18] The interdependence between the optimum tariff and optimum capital tax rates necessitates their joint estimation. It has been concluded that, although either the tariff or the tax rate can be negative, it cannot be that both of them are negative. Yet both of them can be positive.[19]

A final note needs to be raised before we leave the subject of optimal tariff and capital tax rates. It refers to the so-called 'magnification effect'.[20] According to that, returns to factors of production change by a relatively greater amount than do commodity prices. If a country exports both capital and goods or imports both of them, then the two terms of trade move in opposite directions. Thus, the net result on intercountry income distribution will depend on the extent that the magnification effect applies, on the countries' commodity and capital trade, and on the relative factor intensity of goods produced and traded. Also in the presence of the 'magnification effect' the absolute value of optimal tax rate will exceed that of the tariff rate.[21]

## C. INTERDEPENDENCE BETWEEN INTRA- AND INTER-COUNTRY INCOME EFFECTS

First we will deal with the various possibilities on income effects related to the borrowing country.

1. If all the additional income (created by the inflow of capital) or the rents (resulting from advanced technology, superior management, etc.) accrue to the foreign factor suppliers, then no direct intracountry effects occur as long as the following two conditions are met. Prices remain unchanged and full employment prevails. An exception to the direct effects can occur if final product prices facing consumers included, prior to domestic production, excise taxes which are later replaced by tariffs. Such

---

[18] See M. C. Kemp, 'The Gain from International Trade and Investment: A Neo-Heckscher–Ohlin Approach', p. 806.

[19] See R. W. Jones, pp. 14 et seq.

[20] See T. M. Rybszynski, 'Factor Endowments and Relative Commodity Prices', *Económica*, vol. 22 (Nov. 1955).

[21] See R. W. Jones, p. 16.

an outcome will shift earnings from the government to the producers, while relative prices facing the consumer remain the same.

2. If the efficiency caused by the foreign factors of production does not result in higher payments to them but, instead, it reduces product prices, then intracountry income effects occur according to the consumption patterns of the host country nationals. Consumers whose basket of goods is more intensive in foreign capital and/or foreign technology inputs will stand to gain more than others.

3. If higher returns to foreign factors of production spill-over with resulting changes of over-all relative factor prices in the host country (rather than being just foreign factor specific), then the following will occur. Given assumptions on competitive market conditions and factor substitutability, foreign capital inflows utilized in capital intensive industries could lead to relative and absolute increase in the price of capital while symmetrically causing relative *and* absolute decrease in wages.[22]

4. For reasons of loyalty or in the case where higher efficiency or monopoly rents resulting from the presence of foreign inputs are shared partly by the domestic factors of production that participate directly in economic activities with foreign capital and/or technology suppliers, then intra- as well as interfactor income effects will occur. Quite often labour working for foreign subsidiaries obtains higher salaries than the equivalent return paid by national firms.[23]

The above examples refer to the direct effects on host, intracountry income distribution. In the case of transnational enterprises, indirect economic effects on income distribution also exist through the influence that such firms exert on macroeconomic policies of the host government with respect to monetary, fiscal, foreign exchange, and trade considerations. Also indirect effects on income distribution through political considerations are

[22] For a geometrical presentation see H. G. Johnson, 'The Efficiency and Welfare Implications of the International Corporation', pp. 46–7. Johnson related the above to the conclusions reached by Dunning on economic grounds that English capital owners welcome North American capital while British labour is adverse to it. See J. H. Dunning, *The Role of American Investment in the British Economy*, PEP Broadsheet 507 (Feb. 1969).

[23] For example, important economic and political results took place because of the fact that Chilean copper-miners, who worked for foreign-owned firms, used to obtain a multiple of the average wage rate of the country or the earnings of the independent miners.

involved, as demonstrated by the case of ITT's recent attempt to interfere with the internal political developments in Chile.

We come now to cite some of the intracountry income effects for the capital-exporting economy.

1. In the case where capital outflows (and more precisely foreign direct investments) imply an expansive activity, rather than the protection of existing export markets, then capital owners could gain while wage earners could be forgoing similar returns because of the exportation of employment opportunities implied in such capital outflows. In the presence of collective bargaining in labour relations the opportunities of alternative country production through foreign direct investment could prove an important negotiating element in the hands of management and capital owners. The history of the recent U.K. labour strike in the plants of the Ford Motor Company demonstrated the management's intent to use the alternative-production-for-export strategy. Also the plans by foreign subsidiaries in Brazil to increase production for exports of automotive components outside Latin America might not be independent, together with other factors, of the present labour situation in that country.

2. In the case where foreign investment is undertaken as a defensive strategy to protect already existing export markets from *third*-country competition then both capital owners and labour of the capital-exporting country could be obtaining gains. In the absence of such foreign investment, a foreign market could be lost. If, though, investment takes place then enhanced employment opportunities for the home country labour are made available through possible exports of processed inputs to be used by affiliated companies abroad.[24]

3. If on the other hand defensive direct investment takes place so as to protect an export market against the competitive threat of an enterprise with the *same* national origin, then differences exist between firm and home country effects. For the former the analysis is equivalent to number 2 above related to defensive investments. For the home country as a whole, though, equivalent arguments presented in the case of the expansive investments are applicable.

[24] See Committee on Finance, United States Senate, *Implications of Multinational Firms for World Trade and Investment and for U.S. Trade and Labor*, Washington, D.C., Feb. 1973.

## D. CRITICAL ASSUMPTIONS OF THE CAPITAL FLOWS THEORY AND THEIR INAPPLICABILITY IN THE FOREIGN DIRECT INVESTMENT MODEL

Both the analytical framework of capital flows theory as well as the conclusions on intercountry incomes distribution presented in sections A and B above are based on several very restrictive assumptions. The latter have very limited applicability in the actual market and production conditions characterizing intercountry factor and product flows in the context of foreign direct investments as well as their causal determinants. We will be briefly examining some of these assumptions.

Although the analysis presented in earlier pages referred to expanding rather than to stagnant activities or economies, many of the questions raised are of static nature. Furthermore, the answers given are at most related to comparative stationary states. As such many of the dynamic issues involved in product and factor flows are excluded.[25] For example, as discussed on p. 19 growth theory suggests that if technical progress is introduced in the export industry of a country it will tend to worsen that economy's terms of trade. Such a conclusion is correct only as far as *existing* export products are concerned. Yet quite often technical progress is related to the export sector of a country, particularly in the manufacturing sector, through the introduction of *new* products.[26] The low price-elasticity of demand that tends to characterize new products and the absence of many competitors during the initial years of their commercial exploitation could enable an innovator to obtain monopoly rents through appropriate pricing of his exports. The expectation of such rents could stimulate the allocation of further resources for technical innovation both at the firm and country level.[27] Thus, technical progress related to the export sector of new products could improve rather than worsen a country's terms of trade.

[25] For the need of several very restrictive assumptions to handle dynamic problems given existing analytical tools see T. Negishi, 'Foreign Investment and the Long-Run National Advantage', *Economic Record* (Dec. 1965).

[26] See W. Gruber, D. Mehta, and R. Vernon, 'The R & D Factor in International Trade and International Investment of United States Industries', *Journal of Political Economy*, vol. 75, no. 1 (Feb. 1967). Also see OECD studies on *Gaps in Technology*, Paris, 1968.

[27] See for example fiscal treatment on royalty remissions for technology sold abroad as practised by the Japanese government.

The above considerations question another critical assumption implicit in the analysis of sections A and B, namely that of competitive market conditions. Theoretical and empirical analysis related to transnational enterprises, as argued in Chapter I previously, have concluded that the behaviour of such firms can only be understood meaningfully if evaluated within a monopoly or oligopoly model. The concentration indices in both the supply side of foreign direct investments as well as in the market structure of the sectors chosen for investments in the host countries,[28] the size of firms undertaking foreign direct investments,[29] their acquisition and merger processes, their technological managerial and other performance all conduce to a structure where analytical tools related to sector-oligopoly simulation models are much more representative. Although such models involve a high degree of indeterminancy, related to games between adversaries, they provide more meaningful results than maximization models that assume intersectorial uniformity of investment propensities and intrasectorial identity of motives by firms. Furthermore, the price and non-price monopoly effects could constitute a much more important factor of income generation and distribution than factor returns based on competitive markets as implied in most capital flow models. The conclusions reached in such models could, thus, be significantly modified or reversed in the presence of oligopoly.

A hypothesis related to the assumptions on competitive conditions in the capital flow theory, postulates that intercountry differences in returns to capital explain investment flows even in the case of transnational firms.[30] The fact that intercountry interest rate differentials have very limited, and often contradictory, explanatory value in the case of foreign direct investment has long been treated in the literature.[31] The presence of cross-hauling of investments among countries or even in the same sector, and the impression given by the consolidated balance

[28] See W. B. Reddaway, *Effects of U.K. Direct Investment Overseas*, Cambridge University Press, Cambridge, 1967.

[29] See R. Vernon, *Sovereignty at Bay: The Multinational Spread of U.S. Enterprises*, Basic Books, New York, 1971, particularly Chapter I.

[30] An alternative hypothesis has been presented that direct investments will tend to equalize returns to capital among countries intrasectorially while differences will persist intersectorially. See R. E. Caves, 'International Corporation: The Industrial Economics of Foreign Investment', *Economica* (Feb. 1971).

[31] For an excellent analysis on the above see S. Hymer's Ph.D. dissertation.

sheets of transnational firms, that they have larger borrowings from high interest rate countries and that they tend to invest more of their assets in low interest rate countries, as well as related findings, present contradictory evidence on the interest differential theory in the case of direct investments. More meaningful explanations have been based on monopoly or oligopoly models, with related issues of product differentiation and market concentration.[32]

The income-generating and distribution effects of foreign direct investment do not appear as explicit in these alternative, more valid hypotheses as they do in the interest differential one. As a result their income implications are not always sufficiently evaluated. Occasionally, despite the departure from standard capital flow theory—as far as the factors that prompt foreign direct investments are concerned—analysis, related to the alternative hypotheses, returns to rather simple maximization models with respect to income effects both for the firm and the participating countries. We will be dealing more extensively on this matter in the chapters that follow.

In the direct investment model capital might often be one of the least important factors involved. It is not only that foreign direct investors can obtain the largest sources of their funds from the host, 'borrowing' countries.[33] (In this case host countries are, in effect, financing to a great extent the international operations of foreign-owned firms.) Of equal or greater importance is the *collective flow of a set of factors of production* whose scarcity for the firm (like management time) and effects on the host country (like the technology used) can be far more significant than capital. Furthermore, with respect to net income, it is not only that a transnational enterprise should, obviously, be maximizing its global returns rather than those of each one of its corporate units. More so, the mechanisms of income generation and the channels of its remission might depend more on interaffiliate sales of goods and services rather than on the explicitly registered returns to capital invested.[34] Such interaffiliate sales create diverse channels

---

[32] For reference to alternative hypotheses see footnotes, pp. 1–2.

[33] See Celso Furtado *Los Estados Unidos y el Subdesarrollo de América Latina*, Instituto de Estudios Peruanos, Lima, Apr. 1971.

[34] Important conceptual and definitional issues arise on the meaning of the term 'return on investment'. Both the numerator and the denominator of R. O. I. are subject to question where, among others, accounting practices (on capitalization of

of income remission whose relative importance depends on a host
of complex factors, including both home and host country policies
as well as company needs and strategies, some of which will be
examined in Chapter VI below.

Thus product, service, and various forms of capital flows are
involved in foreign direct investments which operate, basically,
within oligopoly markets. As a result a proper understanding of
the behaviour of transnational firms requires analysis that
'belongs more to the theory of industrial organization than that
of international capital movements'.[35] It has also been noted that
'. . . it is not true that these great sums flow abroad as a result of a
free and enlightened calculation of self-interest. They flow as the
result of a particular social organization which . . . gives a bias in
this direction.'[36] The particular 'social organization' of foreign
direct investments by transnational enterprise places the subject
not only outside *the* theory of capital movements but also, to a
great extent, out of *a* theory on capital flows. As such the corresponding analysis requires an understanding of collective factor
utilization across national boundaries under an oligopolistic
market structure. In this context capital itself plays only one part
with, probably, decreasing importance as compared to technology,
managerial competence, marketing techniques and the more
general and not sufficiently analysed considerations of the
economics of knowledge and power.

The chapters that follow analyse some of the elements involved
in intercountry income distribution as a result of company
behaviour stemming from the particular characteristics and power
of transnational firms. First, we will present the results of research
undertaken on the subject in the countries of the Andean Pact.
These findings will later be interpreted within a broader conceptual
framework of government and company policies as well as
industry characteristics.

---

intangibles, international allocation of overheads, declaration of investments as
costs and vice versa depending on pertinent fiscal treatments, etc.) have a critical
importance.
[35] See C. P. Kindleberger, 'Restrictions on Direct Investments in Host Countries'
p. 9.
[36] J. M. Keynes, 'Foreign Investment and National Advantage', p. 585.

CHAPTER III

# Methodology of Empirical Research[1]

In accordance with the conceptual framework presented, the empirical work attempted to bring together the various components that constitute the package of resources exchanged in the foreign direct investment cum technology cum trade model. On the income side, which represented the collective accrual of returns to foreign suppliers of jointly sold inputs, a similar methodological approach was followed. For example, instead of defining reported profits as return to direct foreign investment, interest payments between affiliates as return to capital lent, royalties as payment for technological and other services, interaffiliate charges on intermediates as some representative of the market price equivalent of such inputs, we brought together all elements to which we had access in order to define the corresponding value added which represents the collective return to collectively supplied inputs. The individually reported magnitude for each input has to be understood in terms of over-all company strategy and as an adjustment to home and host government policies and conditions as analysed in Chapters V and VI of the book.

The empirical evaluation included an analysis of data related to:

(1) the volume, prices, origin, etc. of *intermediate products* imported by capital and/or technology receivers, principally in the Colombian pharmaceuticals, electronics, rubber, and basic chemicals industries. Much smaller samples were studied in Chile and Peru (pharmaceuticals) and Ecuador (electronics);

(2) the diverse terms of *technology licensing contracts*, in five countries of the Andean Pact;

(3) the results of negotiations appearing in the *minutes and proceedings* of the Colombian Committee of Royalties;

(4) the financial variables appearing in *company books*, such as

---

[1] The reader not interested in the details of the research requirements concerning our empirical findings can proceed directly to the next chapter.

balance sheets, income statements, statutes of company constitution, etc.;

(5) the elements of *host government policies* which had bearing on our analysis appearing in official publications related to tariff and tax structures, regulations on foreign investment, industrial property laws, restrictive business practices, etc.

The following describes briefly our methodology in each of the above areas:

## (1) *Intermediate product prices*

A critical issue faced from the start was the utility of published information or import statistics for the type of analysis undertaken in this area. All officially published information, and that not published but tabulated, involves families or groups of products. Even six-digit specifications have certain aggregations. Average prices could have been obtained but their use for our comparative purposes might have been misleading. One does not find a meaningful international price for vitamins in general. One does, though, for vitamin $B_{12}$ or vitamin A. The structure of imports and their weighted value will greatly affect either company or country price average and this will greatly influence measurements at the company level. Furthermore, quality differences, whose effects in groups of products will be difficult to differentiate, will make the task of sorting out monopoly rents from payments for improved products impossible.[2] It is not uncommon to find companies whose cost of materials amounts to 25 per cent of sales or more. Also, quite often, reported profits do not exceed 5 per cent of sales. Thus, a 10 per cent difference in the average price of intermediates, which could easily be attributed to quality or to monopoly or to other reasons, will imply, *ceteris paribus*, a 50 per cent change in reported profits. The high elasticity of results with respect to the valorization of inputs required an exact definition of differences in prices which can only be obtained at the product level.

Furthermore, officially published statistics with respect to the country of origin and magnitude of costs of firms (like the data prepared by the U.S. Department of Commerce on the basis of

[2] The debate on the measurement of terms of trade in the 1950s is quite indicative of the difficulties and counterarguments involved in the explanation of price trends at the aggregate level.

company-given information)[3] have important limitations. Such limitations, with respect to intermediate products, stem both from company practices and from the import substitution policies of the host countries. For example, tire manufacturers could declare purchase of semi-processed rubber as a 100 per cent local input since *it* was purchased in the host country. Yet, domestically originated semi-processed rubber could have a high import content of latex and/or natural rubber.

With respect to company practices, the operations of Philips International in Colombia are quite indicative in this matter. Philips has two subsidiaries in that country. One purchases components from its foreign affiliates and sells them to the other. The latter assembles these components to produce electrical consumer durables. A 100 per cent foreign content of intermediates for the first subsidiary will be reduced to 50 per cent in statistics combining both affiliates in Columbia. A study of foreign companies that entered Colombia between 1958 and 1967 indicated that out of 51 new firms of North American origin, on which data were available, 20 were subsidiaries of other foreign subsidiaries already established.[4] Thus production and commercial relationships between affiliates within a country could greatly affect measurement of results.

Given the importance of intermediate products pricing on the basic conclusions of our work and its implications in evaluating the effects of foreign direct investments, it was concluded that published information was of minimal value in our research. Information had to be obtained directly from the origin of corresponding data. A researcher worked for 11 months in the Customs Office and the Instituto de Comercio Exterior of Colombia and from the invoices submitted by the importers to the Custom Office he tabulated information for more than 1,500 different products. The information included (a) name of product; (b) quality specification if any; (c) name of importer; (d) name of exporter; (e) country of exportation; (f) country of initial origin of product; (g) FOB price of product; (h) total volume of importation; (i) import tariffs and dues; (j) import permits and prior

---

[3] See various publications of the Council for Latin America in this respect.
[4] Cited by M. Wionczek in 'Hacia el Establecimiento de un Trato Común para la Inversión Extranjera en el Mercado Común Andino'. *El Trimestre Económico* (México, Apr.–June, 1971), p. 667.

deposits if any. This information was collected for two or three importations for the same product by the same importer in a given year (generally 1968 or 1969) to avoid differences in prices resulting from an atypical importation, or from errors of reporting. (The same methodology together with the corresponding international prices was used by additional researchers in Chile, Peru, and Ecuador as a basis for comparison of selected products in much smaller samples of data.) An economist, working for more than two months, tabulated the above information in Colombia, by company, and selected close to 800 products which accounted for more than 60 per cent of the imports of the companies selected in the different industrial sectors. This work was followed by that of specialists in each industry (i.e. a pharmacologist in the pharmaceutical industry) who examined *each one* of the products selected with respect to possible quality differences given the necessary use. The products about which doubts existed with respect to quality were excluded from the sample. The remaining were products for which quality differences (of all sorts, even packaging in some cases) could not justify more than ± 10 per cent of the FOB price. More specific information by industry will be given below when the sectorial samples are discussed. Once the sample of products were selected they were again tabulated by industry, excluding at this time company names.

After this information was checked, data for FOB prices in different markets in the world were sought for the same products. Such 'international prices' were obtained in the following way:

(a) Five Commercial Attachés of Colombia requested information from companies in the countries of their appointment.
(b) The Customs Office as well as private national firms in Colombia wrote for and obtained price quotations directly from distributors and producers abroad.
(c) One of the researchers in the study was sent for a month to visit European firms and collect prices.
(d) A graduate student at Harvard University collected information from the private sector, university libraries, and government agencies (i.e. U.S. Tariff Commission) in the United States.
(e) Industry publications (such as the *European Chemical News*) were checked to obtain list prices.

(f) Correspondence was sought and prices were obtained from official institutions such as the Malaysian Rubber Exchange.

(g) Price of imports of firms in Colombia (with different capital structures) were tabulated for the same product.

It is estimated that more than one man-year of work was collectively allocated in order to obtain 'international prices'. Obvious cases of dumping were excluded and attempts were made to check in every form possible the validity of the obtained information.

## (2) *Technology contracts*

The contractual terms of technology purchase were obtained from the analysis of 451 contracts in the five Andean countries. In terms of royalty payments the contracts evaluated in Colombia amounted to more than one-third of the country's total, and in Chile, to more than 40 per cent. In Bolivia, most of the known contracts in the manufacturing sector were evaluated, while in Ecuador, access was obtained to only 14 per cent of the contracts deposited in the Central Bank. In Peru, access was limited mostly to contracts in the pharmaceutical sector and to a very few in other industrial activities. In total, material had to be collected, analysed, and tabulated by reading somewhere between 9,000 and 12,000 pages. This was undertaken by five lawyers who served as researchers on the basis of a common methodology after a training period of four weeks. This training was part of an explicit effort to create an infrastructure of government officials who in the future could analyse and negotiate contracts with foreign technology suppliers. The issue researched referred to the typology of the explicit and implicit rights and obligations assumed by both licensors and licensees in contracts of technology purchase. Also, analysis in legal literature was undertaken on types of clauses not usually included in such contracts to the detriment of the licensees.

Despite the fact that the basic methodology pursued was a common one, different administrative and legal requirements existing in the Andean countries prior to their Common Code on Foreign Investments, Patents, Trademarks, and Licensing necessitated diverse procedures so as to obtain the requisite information. Thus, in Chile and Colombia, as a result of prior legislation, contracts of technology commercialization were deposited in corresponding government agencies. In Ecuador, many contracts deposited in the Central Bank were not available for analysis, while in Peru and Bolivia the researchers had to contact the private sector directly. As a result data was not equally available and some of the information not totally comparable. For example, data in Chile and Colombia included the results of some government negotiation with foreign technology suppliers while in the other countries the terms reflected the agreement reached only between private contracting parties.

### (3) *Committee of Royalties*

To understand the dynamics of bargaining, including the learning process of negotiating officials as well as their pursuit and use of information, research was undertaken in the minutes and proceedings of the Colombian Committee of Royalties. In addition, participation took place in the preparation and actual negotiating process related to the approval of various technology contracts. The net effects of bargaining, through the intervention of a government agency, were calculated by comparing the original terms of agreements between Colombian firms and foreign technology suppliers and the alterations achieved after the second negotiation through the Committee of Royalties. Given the changes in the terms of agreement, complementary information was sought from the financial accounts of firms to determine reductions in royalty payments.

### (4) *Financial accounts*

Given the very limited disclosure practices of foreign subsidiaries, as well as of national firms in developing countries (even if such firms are incorporated), diverse sources of information were sought so as to obtain relevant financial information. Balance sheets, income statements, and other financial accounts for firms in Colombia were obtained from five different government agencies which, for reasons of taxation, approval of investments or of technology contracts, balance of payments transactions, etc., included in their files company information. Data were sought on sales, costs of goods sold and their components, as well as the country of accrual of payments, on investments (which had to be translated into constant dollar values given periodic devaluations of the peso), on dividend and royalty remissions, on declared profits, etc. Value-added estimates were undertaken for each of the individual firms for which information was available. The equivalent of four months' research was dedicated to the above.

## (5) *Host government policies*

To complete our understanding of corporate behaviour and its adjustment to government policies, data were collected on government policies with respect to:

(a) tax structures;
(b) tariff levels, prior deposits, and quantitative restrictions in the industries studied;
(c) balance of payment regulations;
(d) foreign investment and technology import regulations;
(e) legislation on industrial property matters;
(f) administrative rules of pertinent government agencies and their formal as well as their operational interdependence, possible conflicting interests, etc.

## *Industry samples*

The following four sectors were studied in Colombia.

(1) *Pharmaceuticals*: this was the sector where most information was available because of the comparatively higher number of contracts related to patents, trademarks, and technical assistance which necessitated government evaluation and approval. This, together with the social effects of the sector, had generated the need for considerable data collection on the part of the Colombian government. On the basis of that data, and additional research we undertook, a sectorial study was developed and part of the conclusions of this study are presented in the book.

Up to about 80 per cent of the Colombian manufacturing pharmaceutical sector is controlled by foreign subsidiaries; the rest is shared by a large number of nationally owned firms. Considerable production concentrations and market segmentation exist by type of product, as a result, to a large extent, of patent privileges and brand names created through high marketing expenditures. Thus, for example, of 20 producers of hormones in Colombia one company controls 45 per cent of the market; of

23 producers of analgesics, 4 control 65 per cent of the market; of 29 producers of vitamins 11 produce more than 80 per cent of the total; of 6 producers of biologics one has more than 75 per cent of that particular market.

We selected for our analysis 17 foreign companies which shared more than 50 per cent of the foreign-controlled market, that is, 40 per cent of the total Colombian market. Also, we selected the 7 largest national firms which accounted for 80 per cent of the nationally controlled market, or 16 per cent of the total. (Most of the other nationally owned firms produce traditional medicines such as balsams and distribute them in their immediate community.)

With respect to our analysis of transfer pricing of raw materials and intermediates, initially information for several hundred products was copied from the Customs Office invoices for this industry. However, several of these products were in substance identical and differed only in name.[5] (Similar practices of intermediate product differentiation through the use of different nomenclatures were noted in the electronics industry as described below.)

A pharmacologist, with fifteen years of experience in the Colombian market, using industry technical catalogues, compared products with respect to dosage and concentration, and identified about 200 different products which accounted for more than 60 per cent of the imports of the firms in the sample. International prices were sought in six European markets and in the U.S.A. for these products, and quotations were obtained for 55 of them. (Solicitations for price quotations for a given product varied between one and eight per product.) Some of these 55 pharmaceutical products were imported by more than one firm and were mainly in the families of antibiotics, hormones and vitamins. They corresponded to a weighted average of about 25 per cent of the reported imports of the foreign subsidiaries in our sample. Also, the products with international price quotations which were used by national firms accounted for about 15 per cent of their total imports. The total annual import volume of the 55 products

---

[5] The case is much more severe in the final product market. The sectorial study mentioned above identified about 15,000 different presentations of pharmaceutical products in the Colombian market. Yet research for the study in the hospital of San Juan de Dios in Bogotá indicated that 120 generic products used were sufficient to cover most of the needs of the hospital in general medicine.

in the sample was on the order of U.S. $5,000,000. Comparisons of these imports and their overpricing with the value added, profit declaration and royalty payments of the importing firms, are given in later chapters. Finally, international prices for 31 of the 55 products were obtained from countries such as Switzerland, West Germany, Denmark, the U.S.A., etc. where patent laws protect at least pharmaceutical processes and in some, like the U.S.A., pharmaceutical products. The remaining 24 were obtained from Italy where patents on pharmaceuticals do not exist. Yet, for these 24 products, prices of 9 of them in Italy were comparable to (sometimes higher than) quotations we received on the same products from other countries with patent legislation covering pharmaceuticals. In those cases where more than two prices were collected per product we never used the lowest for comparison with the FOB prices paid by importing Colombian firms. Rather we used as a base the price that appears in italic figures in the list of product prices presented in Appendix 5.

(2) *Chemicals*: because of the diversity of the chemical industry and the difference that this creates in technological requirements, relative size of fixed assets, import requirements, etc., we excluded from our analysis several categories of chemical products such as the petrochemicals. We included three groups of products which involved the basic chemicals family (such as alkalis, sulphuric and other acids), intermediate chemical products (such as acetates and resins) and final product chemical derivatives (such as paints and pesticides). Seventeen companies were included in the sample, of which five were foreign wholly owned subsidiaries accounting for about 30 per cent of the sales of the respective family of products controlled by foreign firms. Five firms of the joint venture type were included and they accounted for at least 45 per cent of the sector's sales provided by companies of mixed capital. Seven national firms accounted for at least 30 per cent of the sales shared by locally owned firms. The diversity of the products included in this industry (which involves, among others, fertilizers, production of acids, fabrication of synthetic fibres, etc.) meant that no exact figures were possible for the total size of the market. An equally important shortcoming was our inability to determine the comparative share of sales by companies with *diverse* ownership structures. What we were able to achieve, by interviewing government

officials and industry representatives, were some gross estimates of the share that companies had in the total sales of companies with *similar* ownership structures, within the corresponding families of groups of chemicals.

Initially, 56 different products were selected. Price quotations from various markets were obtained for 22 of them. The total volume of imports for these 22 products was on the order of U.S. $6,000,000. For the foreign subsidiaries in the sample, the products on which international prices were obtained accounted for 12 per cent of their total imports. The corresponding percentages for joint ventures and nationally owned firms were 37 per cent and 35 per cent respectively. It is worth noting that the international prices we used were obtained from industry publications such as the *European Chemical News*, *Japan Chemical Review*, and the *Oil, Paint, and Drug Report*. Such publications usually carry list prices from which discounts are granted depending on the volume of purchase. Thus our estimates of overpricing underestimate the true price differential charged to Colombia-based firms.

(3) *Rubber industry*: the Colombian rubber industry is dominated by three foreign-controlled firms that share among them about 80 per cent of the local market. A relatively small national firm has about 5 per cent and several small firms which produce specialty rubber products participate in the remainder. Price quotations were sought for 38 products of synthetic rubber and 8 products of natural rubber totalling about U.S. $5,500,000. Information was obtained only on natural rubber following the weekly quotations of the Malaysian Rubber Exchange. The total volume of imports for which quotations were obtained was rather below U.S. $2,000,000. The corresponding products accounted for more than 60 per cent of the imports of one of the foreign firms in the industry and for more than 80 per cent of those of the principal national firm. It is worth noting that although the origin of natural rubber imported in Colombia was Malaysia, the parent corporation of the foreign firm studied was registered as the intermediate seller of rubber to its Colombian subsidiary. Thus, the effects of transfer pricing for Colombia benefited the home country of the parent.

(4) *Electronics industry*: the sample included in our research for the electronics industry involved mostly products such as

television sets, radios, and record players as well as their components. We did not include products such as refrigerators which, under certain classifications, are included in other industries.

Since the size of the market in Colombia is not known, as a result of considerable illegal entry of electronic products, company shares in the total market could not be estimated. We selected 14 firms for which we were able to obtain, as in the chemical industry, through interviews with government and company officials, gross estimates about the share of production (rather than sales) that the firms in the sample represented in comparison with the production of firms with similar ownership structure. Hence we were not able to obtain information on comparative shares between foreign and national firms. We included four foreign-owned subsidiaries which account for about 40 per cent of the production of foreign firms in Colombia, four joint ventures which account for more than 50 per cent of the corresponding production and six national firms with more than 60 per cent of the production of national firms.

An electronics engineer catalogued all components that comprise close to 90 per cent of the inputs for assembling the corresponding products. The same engineer, with the assistance of industry catalogues, grouped together different nomenclatures that appeared either in import invoices or in company information provided to the Ministry of Development. Prices for the different components were obtained mostly from the U.S.A., Holland, and West Germany, from three sources of information: first, industry quotations; second, information available from U.S. government agencies; and third, from import data of other firms importing in the Colombian market.

# CHAPTER IV

# Empirical Evidence on Monopoly Rents[1]

IN introducing the empirical evidence it appears appropriate to indicate the areas or mechanisms by which resource flows (technology and/or capital) generate or preserve monopoly rents. In doing so we will first present in summary form some of the relevant clauses that exist in a typical contract of technology commercialization. The clauses analysed raise important economic and legal issues regarding the extent to which private contracting and the private economic benefits derived from it, by some or all of the parties involved, are in conflict with the over-all economic and social interests of the country where they operate. Some answers to such questions have long been provided in the industrialized world through anti-monopoly and anti-trust legislation as well as through the establishment of public regulatory agencies. Many developing countries have still to demonstrate an awareness of these issues and their implications for their economic private and public interests. Furthermore, the terms to be discussed below raise questions about the concept of liberty or sovereignty to contract among unequals. In a bargaining structure with highly unequal participants, with limited information and imperfect over-all market conditions, the sovereignty of the 'technology consumers' becomes a concept with very limited applicability.

Typical contracts of technology commercialization between parent and subsidiary in the Andean countries include the following clauses:

(1) *Tie-in clause for intermediate product purchases*: 'For the elaboration of . . . product, covered by article No. . . . in the contract, the licensee is required to purchase all necessary products, [raw materials and intermediate products], as recommended by the licensor, from the source that the licensor indicates'.

---

[1] Some of the figures and analysis of this chapter appeared in C. V. Vaitsos, *Comercialización de Tecnología en el Grupo Andino*, Instituto de Estudios Peruanos, Lima, 1973.

(2) *Tie-in clause for machinery purchases*: 'The installation and any eventual modification or amplification of the licensee's plant will be subject to the approval of the licensor; . . . such purchases for [machinery] will be subject to the licensor's consent.'

(3) *Export restrictive clause*: '. . . the licensee is not permitted to export . . . products as covered by article . . . of the contract.'

(4) *Tie-in clause on personnel*: 'Article . . . obliges the licensee to fabricate the products [covered by the contract] only under the direction of a . . . [professional] selected and trained by the licensor. In addition, article . . . stipulates that the Director of Marketing will be a person trained by the licensor and designated in common accord . . . The remuneration for this professional will be covered by the licensee.'

(5) *Sale or resale clause*: 'In accordance with article . . . of the contract the resale of intermediate products or the sale of products to be produced by the licensee, will be submitted to the prior agreement of the licensor; . . . article . . . stipulates that the prices of sales to the public, will be 'fixed' in common agreement by the two contracting parties . . .'

In evaluating contracts between a foreign wholly owned subsidiary and licensors who are not affiliated with the parent corporation, or contracts between nationally owned firms and foreign licensors, one generally distinguishes two main differences as compared to contracts between parent and subsidiary firms. First, in tie-in arrangements a further provision is introduced which states that '. . . intermediate products have to be purchased from a party designated by the licensor as long as the prices of such products do not differ (or do not differ by more than 10 per cent) from the competitive prices in the world market, given quality specifications.' Second, sale or resale as well as 'price fixing' clauses are not so frequent.

In the five Andean countries 451 contracts belonging to various sectors were evaluated. The country breakdown was as follows:

| Country | No. of contracts | No. of sectors |
|---------|------------------|----------------|
| Bolivia | 35 | 4 including 'others' |
| Colombia | 140 | 4 |
| Chile | 175 | 13 |
| Ecuador | 12 | 5 |
| Peru | 89 | 2 including 'others' |

The economic implications of some of the above-mentioned contractual arrangements, as also affected by non-contractual elements in the system of resource transfers, can be portrayed as follows.

## A. TIE-IN CLAUSES, EFFECTS ON INTERMEDIATE PRODUCT PRICING AND THEIR IMPLICATIONS

A large percentage of the contracts in the commercialization of technology includes obligatory terms which designate the purchase of intermediates and capital goods from the same source as that of know-how. Even in the absence of such explicit terms, control through ownership of technological requirements and specifications, stemming from the nature of the know-how sold, could determine uniquely the source of intermediate products. Thus, as in the case of tie-in arrangements in loans, benefits for the supplier and costs for the purchaser are not limited only to the explicit payments such as royalties or interest rates. They also include implicit charges in various forms of margins in the concomitant or tied sale or other goods and services. Furthermore, at the aggregate level, flows of technology among countries imply directionally the joint flow of intermediates, equipment, and capital.[2]

As far as tie-in arrangements are concerned these take various forms in the contracts of technology commercialization. The majority of them explicitly require the purchase of materials from the technology supplier. Some contracts in addition prohibit, limit or control the use of local materials. Still others can achieve, indirectly, similar results in the purchase of intermediates through quality control clauses. Patents (or trade marks) often strongly affect the tied purchase of materials. The types of technology or intermediate products imported by developing countries have generally several alternative sources of supply if an adequate search for them is undertaken. However, monopoly privileges through patents restrict such supply to the patent holder.

Tie-in clauses on intermediates for Bolivia, Ecuador, and Peru appeared as given in Table IV, 1, which demonstrates that 67 *per cent of the contracts with relevant information had tie-in clauses*

---

[2] For a fuller analysis on this last point see W. Gruber, D. Mehta, and R. Vernon, 'The R & D Factor in International Trade and International Investment of United States Industry', *Journal of Political Economy* (Fall, 1966).

TABLE IV. 1

| Country | Total contracts | Contracts with explicit tie-in clauses | Contracts explicitly permitting free importation |
|---|---|---|---|
| Bolivia | 35 | 29 | 6 |
| Ecuador | 12 | 8 | 4 |
| Peru | 89 | 55 | 34 |
| Total | 136 | 92 | 44 |

*in these countries.* The industry break-down in Bolivia was as given in Table IV. 2.

TABLE IV. 2

| Sector | Contracts with explicit tie-in clauses | Contracts explicitly permitting free importation |
|---|---|---|
| Food and beverages | 11 | 0 |
| Textiles | 4 | 3 |
| Pharmaceuticals | 4 | 1 |
| Others | 10 | 2 |

In Colombia, 100 per cent of the contracts of foreign-owned subsidiaries and above 95 per cent of nationally owned firms in the pharmaceutical industry included tie-in clauses. In the Colombian chemical industry three out of five contracts had such clauses. In all countries it appeared that the pharmaceutical industry had the highest or among the highest percentages of tie-in arrangements.

The implications of these explicit tie-in arrangements, as well as the implicit ones that result from ownership ties among affiliates, become particularly acute for developing countries if one takes into account the *increasing* dependence of their economies on the importation of intermediate products and capital goods as they advance in the first stages of their industrialization. For example, in Colombia two-thirds of the total import bill in 1968 comprised imports of materials, machinery, and equipment for the industrial sector while the other third included final products for consumption and intermediate goods for the agricultural sector.[3] Similar

[3] See data from Banco de la República, tabulated by INCOMEX *Clasificación Económica de las Importaciones*, Colombia, 1969.

dependence and structure of imports is to be expected for Chile and Peru and other nations of comparable industrial development. Also Bolivia and Ecuador, following the same road (particularly in the manufacturing sector), are likely to find an increasing dependence on imports of intermediates and capital goods as their industrialization advances. For the whole of Latin America it has been estimated that during the period 1960–5 about U.S. $1,870 millions were spent annually for the importation of machinery and equipment. These imports amounted to 31 per cent of the total import bill of the area. They also constituted about 45 per cent of the total amount spent by Latin America on capital goods during the same period. For individual countries this relationship amounted to 28 per cent for Argentina, 35 per cent for Brazil, 61 per cent for Colombia, and 80 per cent for Chile. It is significant to note that about one-third of the total imports of machinery and equipment in Latin America is realized by foreign subsidiaries.[4] As far as intermediates are concerned, industry samples in Colombia have indicated that imported materials represented in 1968 between 52 per cent and 80 per cent of total materials used by firms in parts of the chemical industry. In rubber products the corresponding ratio was 57·5 per cent, and in pharmaceuticals 76·7 per cent. It was only in textiles that the ratio of imported intermediates to total materials used fell to 2·5 per cent. Similar figures were reported for Chile. For example, imported intermediate products amounted to more than 80 per cent of total materials used in the pharmaceutical industry and between 35 per cent and 50 per cent of total sales of the firms involved.

Defining as overpricing:

$$\frac{\left(\begin{array}{c}\text{FOB price paid by}\\\text{purchasing nation}\end{array}\right) - \left(\begin{array}{c}\text{FOB prices quoted in different}\\\text{markets around the world}\end{array}\right)}{\left(\begin{array}{c}\text{FOB prices quoted in different markets}\\\text{around the world}\end{array}\right)} \times 100$$

Our research in Colombia indicated the results shown in Table IV.3.

[4] Preliminary estimates by CEPAL presented by F. Fanjzilber, *Elementos para la Formulación de Estrategias de Exportación de Manufacturas*, ST/ECLA/Conf. 3/L.21, Santiago, Chile, July 1971, pp. 91–5.

## TABLE IV. 3

| Ownership structure | Pharmaceutical industry | | | Rubber industry | | | Chemical industry | | | Electronics industry | | |
|---|---|---|---|---|---|---|---|---|---|---|---|---|
| | a % | b % | c* % | a % | b % | c % | a % | b % | c % | a % | b % | c % |
| Foreign-owned | 50 | 25 | 155 | 33 | 60 | 40 | 30 | 12 | 25·5 | 40 | 90 | 16–60 |
| Joint ventures | n.a. | n.a. | n.a. | n.a. | n.a. | n.a. | 45 | 37 | 20·2 | 50 | 90 | 6–50 |
| Nationally owned | 80 | 15 | 19 | 80 | 60 | 0 | 30 | 35 | 22·2 | 60 | 90 | 25–69 |

* Individual firm data is as follows: 'Overpricing' for firm #1: 253·6%; #2: 133·7%; #3: 132·8%; #4: 306·2%; #5: 483·%; #6: 39·5%; #7: 179·4%; #8: 79·1%; #9: 58·3%; #10: 73·8%; #11: 475·4%; #12: 374·7%; #13: 177·5%; #14: 164·8%; #15: 60·4%; #16: 476·9%: #17: 34·4%.

Index a: Approximate percentage of sales by firms included in the sample as compared to total sales of firms with *similar* capital structure in the Colombian market. As indicated in the previous chapter it was not possible to estimate for the chemical and electronics industries the exact share of the market for firms of *different* capital structures. For consistency we kept this distinction for the pharmaceutical and rubber industries although more precise figures were obtained for these industries. For exact information see sample description presented in the previous chapter.

b: Total volume of imports evaluated as a percentage of the firms' total importation.

c: Weighted average of overpricing of evaluated products for all industries except in electronics where it was possible to estimate only ranges of occurring overpricing.

n.a.: not available.

The dollar value of the overpricing in pharmaceuticals amounted to approximately U.S. $3,000,000. About 50 per cent of this would have been taxed by the Colombian government if it had been declared as profits at the subsidiary level. Of the remainder, the largest percentage, perhaps as high as 70 per cent or more, would legally also have remained in the host country since the companies would have reached the limit of permissible repatriated profits with only a small part of the amount paid through overpricing. Thus about 50 per cent of the total amount represents a fiscal loss for the Colombian government, and above

80 per cent of it, a balance of payments loss.[5] It is of interest to mention here the triangular form of the intermediate product flow of several of these companies. Although the origin of the products was European or U.S., they were sold to Colombia via Panama through the intervention of a holding company. Thus, the difference between the price charged to Colombia and the original cost of these products was passed to a tax jurisdiction which used to be a tax haven for U.S. firms, and continues partly to be so nowadays for them, and totally for several European firms.

At this point one can reflect on some hypothetical cases. If the evaluated pharmaceutical companies pursue the same pricing practices (155 per cent overpricing on the average) for the importation of the rest of their products, then the total over-pricing charge will be more than U.S. $10,000,000 for 1968. (*A priori* there is no reason why the rest of the products will be more or less overpriced. Data were collected on the basis of quotations that we obtained on 'international prices'.) Also if the other half of the pharmaceutical industry is also practising, on the average, the same overpricing policies, then the total charge to the Colombian balance of payments for 1968 will amount to more than U.S. $20,000,000 just from the pharma-ceutical sector. This figure is at the order of magnitude of, or perhaps more than, all the annual known explicit payments (royalties) for industrial technology by the whole economy of Colombia. If for any possible reason our figures of overpricing are under or over-estimated, the comparison between foreign-owned subsidiaries and nationally owned firms in the Colombian pharmaceutical industry clearly indicates that, using the same basis of information, overpricing differed in percentage terms by a multiple of more than seven times on the average between the two classes of firms.

The fiscal loss and balance of payments burden for the economy from the overpricing of the evaluated rubber products were in figures of hundreds of thousands of U.S. dollars for 1968. For the chemical industry the immediate balance of payments charge to the economy amounted to close to U.S. $1,300,000 and the fiscal loss for the government was over U.S. $600,000.

[5] From the fiscal loss resulting from overpricing one has to subtract the revenues accruing to the government through higher tariff payments because of such over-pricing.

The smaller samples studied in other countries of the Andean Pact for the pharmaceutical industry do not permit extrapolation of the estimates obtained nor any estimates of weighted averages. The absolute figures of these studies were reported as follows.

In Chile from 50 products for which international prices were available corresponding to the imports of 39 firms:

11 products reported no overpricing;
9 products reported overpricing between 1% and 30%;
14 products reported overpricing between 31% and 100%;
12 products reported overpricing between 101% and 500%;
2 products reported overpricing above 500%;
In terms of ownership structure of the importing firms:
0–30% overpricing was reported in 13 nationally owned firms and in 6 foreign-owned;
31–100% overpricing was reported in 13 nationally owned firms and in 3 foreign-owned;
100%+ overpricing was reported in 2 nationally owned firms and in 10 foreign-owned.

In Peru prices corresponding to imports of 22 firms were studied with the results given in Table IV. 4.

TABLE IV. 4

| Percentage of overpricing | No. of national-owned firms reporting such overpricing | No. of foreign-owned firms reporting such overpricing |
|---|---|---|
| 0–20 | 4 | 3 |
| 20–50 | 1 | 5 |
| 50–100 | 1 | 2 |
| 100–200 | 1 | 2 |
| 200–300 | 0 | 2 |
| 300+ | 0 | 1 |

(Recent unpublished work by an agency of the Colombian government has indicated that some of our estimates in the pharmaceutical industry underestimated the magnitude of overpricing of intermediate product imports by foreign subsidiaries.[6])

Another industry studied outside Colombia was that of

[6] For comparison of the Chilean, Peruvian, and Colombian pharmaceutical sectors see P. Díaz, 'Análisis Comparativo de los Contratos de Licencia en el Grupo Andino', mim., Lima, Sept. 1971, pp. 19–28.

electronics in Ecuador. An analysis of 29 different imported intermediate products in the latter country indicated the following: sixteen were imported at prices comparable to those of Colombia; seven had an overpricing up to 75 per cent and six of them had rates of overpricing of about 200 per cent. Thus the percentages of overpricing in electronics for Colombia have to be adjusted upwards in the corresponding products for Ecuador.

In summary the main industries we studied with respect to the pricing practices of firms on imported intermediate products were the pharmaceuticals (in Colombia, Chile, and Peru) and the electronics (in Colombia and Ecuador). A relatively smaller number of products was studied in the chemical and rubber industries (in Colombia). In all sectors and countries that were evaluated, significant returns to foreign factors of production appeared to accrue through the profit margins of products tied into the importation of capital and/or technology. By far the highest rates of overpricing were noted in the pharmaceutical industry.[7]

In all countries studied, overpricing on products imported by foreign-owned subsidiaries was in general higher (and in certain industries considerably higher) than that of nationally owned firms. Foreign subsidiaries in the cases investigated apparently use transfer pricing of products as a mechanism of income remission, thus significantly understating their true profitability. Signs of similar behaviour can also be seen in other industries which we did not study in depth. For example, a large part of the automotive industry in the Andean Pact has been declaring losses over several years. (The high effective protection could possibly more than compensate for the inefficiency of small-scale production.) Despite the declared losses by existing firms new ones are eager to enter. In Colombia, although the existing firm (Chrysler Co.) reported losses for several consecutive years, about 14 new companies requested production permits in 1969. Also during efforts undertaken by governments to rationalize production in the automotive industry in the Andean Pact, practically all existing manufacturers, despite their declared losses, presented requests to continue their assembly plants.

[7] For specific information related to the profitability of this industry in another country see United States Senate, *Comparative Problems in the Drug Industry*, Hearings before the Subcommittee on Monopoly, 1959 and following years.

In cases of imports of products in developing countries, returns to the foreign factor suppliers are realized, among others, through the *over*pricing of such products. In cases of exports of products from a country, similar returns can be realized through the *under*pricing of the products sold from companies to their foreign affiliates. Preliminary research in Colombia, still in progress, has given indication of significant underpricing of exports by foreign subsidiaries to their parents in the timber, fish-processing, and precious metals industries. Similarly, foreign industrialists with an interest in entering the fishing industry in Peru have expressed their preference of breaking even, in their operations in Peru, while making their profits 'in the marketing end abroad'.

We pass now to a brief analysis of tie-in arrangements of machinery and equipment in capital and/or technology transfers. Again here, resource and product flows generally take place in a package form where both benefits and costs have to be evaluated in a way in which the lowest reducible unit is a collective one. The case of turn-key factories built by suppliers of equipment is an exemplary demonstration of how technology commercialization can be completely embodied in the sale of equipment of fully armed factories. Also capital transfers depend on the magnitude of real transfers through the sale of capital goods (i.e. in 1968 about 64 per cent of the total uses of funds by U.S. affiliates were devoted to property, plant, and equipment,[8] a considerable part of this could have been imported from the capital-supplying country). A sampling of five of the largest foreign-owned firms in the Colombian chemical industry indicated that on the average about 50 per cent of the initial investment was in the form of capitalization of equipment.[9] Moreover, in the rubber industry, information available for one of the three foreign firms in the country indicated that about 40 per cent of the initial investment was in the form of capital goods.[10]

The present research work did not attempt to collect information on prices of machinery imported into Colombia. It appears that such an investigation would have needed an allocation of

[8] See U.S. Department of Commerce, *Survey of Current Business*, 'Sources and Uses of Funds of Foreign Affiliates of U.S. Firms, 1967–68', Nov. 1970, pp. 16–17.

[9] From unpublished information from the Banco de la República and the Comité de Regalías of the Government of Colombia.

[10] From unpublished information from the Banco de la República and the Comité de Regalías of the Government of Colombia.

considerably more time and effort than was available to us. The market of specialized equipment, with small variations in design or component parts drastically affecting prices, is not as easy to evaluate as the market for natural rubber or sodium phosphate. In addition, since a considerable part of the machinery imported is second-hand,[11] several definitional and arbitrary questions are raised about what is a fair price. Yet it appears that in all of the few cases where Colombia government officials were able to scrutinize the prices of capital goods (capitalized or bought) there was considerable overpricing by the foreign suppliers of equipment who happened, at the same time, to be capital and/or technology transferrers.[12]

A significant point needs, furthermore, to be added. The above-cited investigations and their results were based on comparisons of overpricing or discriminatory pricing, which in turn imply the comparison between two different prices. Yet income flows occur on the basis of *pricing* and not just on overpricing. The former implies the comparison between price and costs, while the latter implies that between prices. In addition to aspects of relative magnitude, important conceptual and measurement considerations are involved. It has been correctly pointed out that there is no such thing as an international market for Volkswagen doors for estimating overpricing.[13] Similarly, there is no world price for a revolving typewriter ball for Olivetti office equipment. In areas of standardized products, such as natural or synthetic rubber, certain chemicals, specific synthetic fibres, nomenclatures of various electronic components, etc., overpricing is an attain-

---

[11] For data on Puerto Rico see W. P. Strassmann, *Technological Change & Economic Development*, Cornell University Press, Ithaca, N.Y., 1968.

[12] A foreign parent corporation, for example, was selling to its own subsidiary machinery at 30% higher prices than the same machinery sold by the same parent to a Colombian competitor of its subsidiary. Another foreign company, in the extractive industry, applied for an import permit for machinery initially valued at U.S. $1,800,000. When the responsible government agency evaluated the procedures by which this figure was reached, it discovered that its value was only U.S. $1,200,000.

Another foreign company in the paper industry applied for the importation of used machinery which, it claimed, was worth US $1,200,000. When the responsible government agency asked for quotations on new models of the same machinery in in the 'international' market, the highest price was U.S. $800,000.

[13] See Charles Cooper for 'Transfer of Technology from Advanced to Developing Countries', study prepared for the Secretariats of ACAST and UNCTAD, Nov. 1970.

able estimate. But, in cases of highly differentiated goods, attempts at estimates are extremely difficult and, in practice, probably meaningless. Furthermore, one can ask what is the relevance of overpricing in the case of a monopoly or a cartel market structure where prices or mark-ups are fixed accordingly. The comparison between prices and costs to determine net generated income begs the question of what are the costs. How should overheads be allocated at the international level? To put the question in a cruder form, and in a manner that leads to value judgements, one can ask: how far should a country (in our case a developing country) contribute not only to the financial, entrepreneurial, and monopoly rents of a transnational enterprise, but also to the coverage of fixed costs of goods and services obtained by it and the parent *as well as* the rest of the world?

The above conceptually perplexing questions do not imply the absence of practical solutions, even if they are partial. They suggest, though, that foreign direct investments fall basically within a *bargaining model* and not, as they are traditionally defined, within a one-sided benefit–cost analysis applied generally to the host country. (We will deal with some of these issues in a later chapter.)

Considerable interest has been raised in the past about the worsening terms of trade in developing countries resulting from their specialization in the production and exportation of primary products. It is not improbable that the present process of industrialization, given the existing mechanisms of technology and foreign capital supply, could result in a further worsening of terms of trade for these countries. Such a deterioration might occur as a result of the fact that the markets within which factors of production (such as technology and capital) are being traded, *jointly with intermediate products and capital goods*, are even more imperfect than the markets of final industrial products. The following figures are presented as an example of the importance of pricing of intermediate products and capital goods which are taking an ever-increasing share in the import bill of many developing countries: Colombia had a total import bill in 1968 which exceeded U.S. $620 millions.[14] From this, if one excludes durable and non-durable consumer products, combustibles,

[14] Source: data from Banco de la República tabulated by INCOMEX, *Clasificación Económica de las Importaciones*, Colombia, 1969.

lubricants, and connected products, raw materials, intermediate products, and capital goods for agriculture, construction materials, transportation equipment, etc., the remaining reflects raw materials, intermediate and capital goods for industry which amounted to close to U.S. $400 millions (close to 25 per cent of which reflected importation of chemical and pharmaceutical products). Some of these products, as indicated in previous pages, included heavy monopoly elements resulting in considerable price differentials in comparison with international prices. Others have lesser monopoly elements and still others probably none. *If Colombia could have reduced the prices of her intermediate products and capital goods on the average by 20 per cent then she could have 'saved' in 1968 foreign exchange equivalents to more than 50 per cent of all her exports other than coffee and petroleum.*

## B. EXPORT RESTRICTIVE CLAUSES

One of the most frequent clauses encountered in contracts of technology commercialization is that of export prohibition. Such restrictive practices generally limit the production and sale of goods utilizing foreign technology solely within the national boundaries of the receiving country. Some allow exports only to specific neighbouring countries. From the total of 451 contracts evaluated in the Andean Pact, 409 contained information on exports which appeared as given in Table IV. 5.

### TABLE IV. 5

| Country | Total number of contracts | Total prohibition of exports | Exports permitted only in certain areas | Exports permitted to the rest of the world |
|---------|---------------------------|------------------------------|------------------------------------------|--------------------------------------------|
| Bolivia | 35 | 27 | 2 | 6 |
| Colombia | 117 | 90 | 2 | 25 |
| Ecuador | 12 | 9 | — | 3 |
| Peru | 83 | 74 | 8 | 1 |
| Total | 247 | 200 | 12 | 35 |

In Chile from 162 contracts with information on the matter 117 prohibited totally any form of exportation. Of the remaining 45 the majority limited export permission to certain countries. It was not possible to estimate the exact number of these partial export permits from the data offered by Chile. Thus, in the four countries where precise figures were available about 81 *per cent of the contracts prohibited exports totally and 86 per cent had some restrictive clause on exports.* In Chile more than 72 per cent of the contracts prohibited exports totally.

The country breakdown in Bolivia, Colombia, and Peru by sector and by ownership structure of the contracts containing information on possibilities of exports of goods utilizing purchased technology can be seen in Table IV. 6.

TABLE IV. 6

| | | Countries | | | | | | | | |
|---|---|---|---|---|---|---|---|---|---|---|
| | | Colombia | | | Bolivia | | | Peru | | |
| Sectors | Ownership structures | Exports prohibited | Partial permission | No export restriction | Exports prohibited | Partial permission | No export restriction | Exports prohibited | Partial permission | No export restriction |
| Textiles | Foreign Wholly owned joint ventures national firms | 11 | 0 | 1 | 4 | 2 | 1 | | | |
| Pharma-ceuticals | Foreign | 31 | 2 | 13 | 1 | 0 | 1 | 13 | 5 | 0 |
| | Joint ventures | 3 | 0 | 0 | | | | | | |
| | National | 34 | 0 | 4 | 3 | 0 | 1 | 52 | 0 | 0 |
| Chemicals | Foreign | 3 | 0 | 2 | | | | | | |
| | joint ventures | 2 | 0 | 2 | | | | | | |
| | National | 6 | 0 | 3 | | | | | | |
| Food and beverages | Foreign | | | | 8 | 0 | 2 | | | |
| | National | | | | 0 | 0 | 1 | | | |
| Others | Foreign | | | | 10 | 0 | 1 | 5 | 1 | 1 |
| | Joint ventures | | | | | | | 1 | 0 | 0 |
| | National | | | | 1 | 0 | 0 | 3 | 2 | 0 |

Interpretation of the data in Table IV. 6 indicates that no significant differences exist among countries. For example, contracts with complete prohibition of exports were the following percentages of the total number of contracts with relevant information:

| | |
|---|---|
| Bolivia | 77% |
| Chile | 72% |
| Colombia | 77% |
| Ecuador | 75% |
| Peru | 89% |

With the exception of Peru where figures were biased upwards by the large number of cases belonging to the pharmaceutical sector in the sample taken, the rest indicate similar percentages in the seventies.

In terms of sectorial comparisons the following figures were noted in the Andean countries with respect to the number of contracts that included some form of export restriction (complete or partial) as a percentage of the total contracts with relevant information:[15]

| | |
|---|---|
| Textiles | 88% |
| Pharmaceuticals | 89% |
| Chemicals | 78% |
| Food and Beverages | 73% |
| Others | 91% |

The above percentages indicate no major differences by sectors. Irrespective of industrial activity, technology suppliers to the Andean group limit possibilities of exports. Such restrictive practices could be explained if the technology suppliers wanted to maintain certain quality standards and control over the corresponding products with respect to specifications, properties, or image to the consumers, etc. Such requirements become critical, once, in addition to or jointly with patent and know-how contracts, trade-mark licensing is introduced. In these cases the licensees might use in foreign markets the name of the licensors and the goodwill that this carries with it. The usage of intangible assets, like the trade name of the products of a firm, by another company could justify control over its effects and image by the (intangible) property owner. Yet, in all export restrictive clauses studied no additional reference was made to quality standards. Rather the prohibition was complete and unconditional. Furthermore, only two references were encountered (both of them in Colombia) on the usage and requirements of trademarks and the possibility of exporting without them. In any case, as will be seen later, quality control of goods produced by the licensees often remained under the licensors.

In terms of ownership structure the following percentages were noted in the Andean countries on the various forms of export

[15] In chemicals we added to the figures of Bolivia, Colombia, Ecuador, and Peru those provided by Chile which included 51 contracts, with complete export prohibitions out of a total of 62 contracts. The rest of the percentages refer only to the former 4 countries.

restrictions with respect to the total number of contracts providing relevant information:

| | |
|---|---|
| Foreign wholly-owned subsidiaries: | 79% |
| Nationally owned firms: | 92% |

It should be noted that such a high percentage of export prohibitive clauses in contracts of technology acquisition by nationally owned firms existed at a time when the Andean nations, with the establishment of their common market, were trying to integrate their economies by, among other policies, increasing intercountry trade. Agreements reached between governments are in the case of technology commercialization greatly conditioned by the terms reached among private firms whose relative bargaining power is totally unequal. Also efforts by UNCTAD and individual governments to achieve preferential treatments for the exports of manufacturing goods from developing countries have to be considered within a market structure which does not permit such exports through explicit restrictive clauses.[16]

Analysis of trade patterns has indicated the increasing importance of technology-embodying products in the total volume of traded goods.[17] Developing countries appear to be left outside the more dynamic sectors of trade, not only because they do not develop or copy technology adequately, nor because their enterprises are relatively small with limited export horizons, etc., but also because when they acquire technology, even belatedly, contractual terms prohibit such exports. For example, in the Colombian textile industry, all nationally owned firms we studied which had export prohibitive clauses in their contracts with foreign technology suppliers, were exporting other products to different countries around the globe. Import substitution by developing countries appears to be a strategy which is not exclusive to their governments but which is also pursued by transnational corporations. Market cartelization and the resulting monopoly rents appear to constitute an objective from which

[16] Frequent export restrictive practices have been observed by the governments of Iran, El Salvador, México, Chile, India, Colombia, Philippines, Kuwait, etc., in the process of purchase of foreign technology. See UNCTAD, *Restrictive Business Practices*, TD/B/C2/93, Dec. 1969, pp. 4–6.

[17] See, for example, W. Gruber, D. Mehta and R. Vernon, 'The R & D Factor in International Trade & International Investment of United States Industry'.

considerable private returns could accrue. However, as the experience of the Latin American Free Trade Association has shown, some companies are more willing to integrate markets than the host governments where they operate.

Obviously the nonexistence of export prohibitive clauses does not necessarily mean the realization of exports. It all depends upon the productive and marketing capacities of the firms, their relative competitive position in external markets, their export horizon, etc. Yet contractually assumed export possibilities, even if they do not constitute a sufficient condition, represent a necessary one for such export capabilities. Moreover, they can create a critical prohibitive element in the long process necessary for firms to develop export orientation and capacities.

The lower percentage figure of export prohibitions noted for foreign wholly owned subsidiaries is of limited significance since control through ownership can dictate export possibilities. Implicit or explicit export limitations on the operations of wholly owned affiliates could appear contradictory. Reasons of efficiency would clearly dictate that the parent corporation will maximize profits by expanding production and sales from the most efficient subsidiary rather than, possibly, prohibiting such action through export restrictive clauses. This might not, though, be so if losses of efficiency were more than compensated by gains in monopoly rents. The costs of loss of efficiency have to be evaluated together with the gains that might accrue through market segmentation and monopoly prices. Thus, export restrictive clauses might be linked to royalty payments. A parent corporation could, for example, reach collectively better terms by negotiating royalty payments for each one of its subsidiaries separately with the Colombian, Chilean, and Mexican governments one at a time, rather than by negotiating with one of them for the markets of all three countries. Monopoly benefits (in this case royalties) can be maximized through spatial segmentation and exploitation of different elasticities of demand rather than through non-discriminatory monopoly pricing. It could be that a firm negotiating with government $A$ could achieve higher royalty payments if it exports from $A$ to countries $B$ and $C$ rather than if it limits its sales only to $A$. Yet this increase might still be smaller than the royalty agreements with countries $B$ and $C$, where demand for technology is more inelastic. Such discriminatory monopoly benefits could, in turn, more than compensate increased costs due to production in less efficient subsidiaries.

A further explanation needs to be given as to why a parent needs to impose explicit export restrictive clauses upon its wholly owned subsidiary, if the same result can accrue from control through ownership. The answers could be various: (1) the parent might need an export restrictive clause so as to hedge against future loss of control in case it decides to sell the subsidiary; (2) an export restrictive clause could provide a legal base to refuse local government's pressures to export (i.e. the French and Japanese governments explicitly request foreign technology suppliers to export from their countries); (3) such restrictions could set clear the rules for local managers who might have pursued policies contrary to the global interests of the parent.

Export prohibitive clauses are clearly beyond the privileges implicit in legal 'captivity' of technology, such as patents.[18] More so, they are illegal under various anti-trust legislation[19] and against specific binational[20] or multinational[21] agreements undertaken by developed countries in the protection of their own interests. Although it is quite difficult to quantify the monopoly benefits that accrue, from such restrictions, to the licensors (or the costs for the licensees), they are, no doubt, potentially of equal or greater value than several of the earlier quantified monopoly elements.

## C. OTHER TYPES OF RESTRICTIVE CLAUSES

To understand the meaning and repercussions of a contract, one has to evaluate it in its totality. Often terms that are defined in clause No. $x$ are conditioned or modified in clause No. $y$. Also, without explicitly stating something so as not to violate local legislation one can achieve pursued ends through indirect,

[18] See definition and analysis of privileges resulting from a patent, as specified by the Commission of the European Common Market, in United Nations, *The Role of Patents in the Transfer of Technology*, New York, 1964, pp. 29–33.

[19] Also see Article 37 of the 1945 Price Ordinance of France. Also Economic Competition Act of 1958 of the Netherlands. Also Restrictive Trade Practices Act of 1956, Part I, of the United Kingdom.

[20] For example '. . . patent rights, granted by a U.S. or Japanese parent are only co-extensive with the geographical limits of the country and do not justify any agreement by a licensee not to export the patented product from the country, which has been held illegal under the laws of those two countries', United Nations. *The Role of Patents*, pp. 29–30.

[21] See Article 85 (1) of the Rome Treaty, 1957.

legally accepted means. For example, through certain quality clauses one can indirectly affect volume of production or control sources of intermediates. Or through control of the volume of production (which is permissible under certain patent legislation) one can control the volume of exports (which is not permitted by the same patent legislations).

Restrictive clauses in contracts of technology commercialization are of various types. For example, in Bolivia out of 35 contracts analysed (and in addition to the export restrictions and tie-in clauses on intermediates cited above) the following terms were included: 24 contracts tied technical assistance to the usage of patents or trade-marks and vice versa: 22 tied additional know-how needed to the present contracts; 3 fixed prices of final goods; 11 prohibited production or sale of similar products; 19 required secrecy on know-how during the contract and 16 after the end of the contract; 5 specified that any controversy or arbitration should be settled in the courts of the country of the licensor. Also, 28 out of the 35 cases contractually set quality control under the licensor. Similarly in Chile out of 175 contracts 98 had quality control clauses under the licensor, 45 controlled the volume of sales and 27 the volume of production. In Peru out of 89 contracts, 66 controlled the volume of sales of the licensee. Some clauses prohibited the sale of similar or the same products after the end of the contract. Others tied the sale of technology to the appointment of key personnel by the licensor.

The list of clauses included in contracts of technology commercialization and the impact they have on business decisions prompt the question: what crucial policies are left under the control of the ownership or management of the recipient firm? If the volume, markets, prices, and quality of what a firm sells, if the sources, prices, and quality of its intermediates and capital goods, if the key personnel to be hired, the type of technology used, etc., if all of these are left under the control of the licensor then the only basic decision left to the licensee is whether or not to enter in an agreement of technology purchase. Technology through the present process of its commercialization, becomes thus a mechanism of control of the recipient firms. Such control supersedes or complements that which results from ownership of the capital of a firm. Political and economic pre-occupations that have been voiced in developing countries concerning the high degree of foreign control of domestic industry can properly be evaluated not only within the foreign direct investment model but also within the mechanism of technology commercialization.

An additional issue needs, furthermore, to be mentioned. The type of clauses encountered in contracts of technology commercialization violate basic anti-monopoly or anti-trust legislation in the home countries of the licensors. Since the extra-territoriality of laws is in general very limited or not applicable it befits the technology-receiving countries to legislate and regulate accordingly so as to protect the interests of the purchasing firms. As indicated in previous pages, industrialized countries have in the last half-century, or even earlier, undertaken to define in one way or another in their legal structure the extent that private contracting and the exercise of business power can operate within a market mechanism.

## D. SOME IMPLICATIONS AND FURTHER EMPIRICAL EVIDENCE

The viewing of resource flows under the light of monopoly rents within collective units of primary inputs and intermediate as well as capital goods has certain distinct implications for the measurements of the effects of foreign direct investment in a country as well as for the investor.

1. Official publications and a great deal of economic analysis limit themselves to the publication or evaluation of profitability resulting from foreign investments as reported in declared profits at the subsidiary level.[22] This, in a system of collective resource flows, could grossly understate the effective profitability resulting from foreign operations. Such understatement and evaluation of published information in their present form logically lead to inferences or conclusions such as the following: '. . . in a well functioning capital market, the gross yield differential between domestic and foreign manufacturing investments is so narrow U.S. return on investment domestically after tax was 13% in 1965 and from U.S. affiliates abroad before tax 11·9%) that tax differentials may have a decisive effect on the net profitability of a

[22] See U.S. Department of Commerce, *Survey of Current Business*, vol. 45, no. 9 (Sept. 1965), pp. 22–31, vol. 46, no. 9 (Sept. 1966), pp. 30–9, etc.

substantial volume of manufacturing investments.'[23] But what profitability should one take into consideration, the reported or the effective?

About 40 per cent of the pharmaceutical industry in Colombia, all foreign wholly owned subsidiaries, reported in 1968 a 6·7 per cent return on investment on the basis of declared profits.[24] If one defines as effective profitability, accruing to the foreign resource transferrer, the declared profits plus royalty payment plus the overpricing of intermediate products imported by the subsidiary, the extrapolated (given our sample of intermediate product prices) effective return on net worth including reinvested profits was 136·3 per cent[25] for the whole 40 per cent of the sector we evaluated. Reported profits were U.S. $361,749 royalty payments to the parent corporation about U.S. $1,472,833 and overpricing of intermediate products about U.S. $8,692,584. In other words, defining as effective returns to the parent corporation the sum of reported profits at the subsidiary, royalty payments, and intermediate products overpricing, and excluding interest payments on interaffiliate loans, the following data can be inferred from our sample representing almost half of the Colombia pharmaceutical industry: *reported profits constitute 3·4 per cent of the effective returns, royalties 14 per cent and overpricing 82·6 per cent.*

If one compares effective profitability with constant value dollars of capital invested by the parent corporations during all previous years, the R. O. I. for 1968 alone was 79·1 per cent for the same industry. The foreign wholly owned subsidiary in the rubber industry, for which data were available, reported at 16 per cent R. O. I. on constant dollars that were imported during all previous time periods in Colombia. The effective rate of return was 43 per cent on the same constant dollars. In the electronics industry a foreign-owned subsidiary declared in 1967 a minus 18 per cent return on net worth due to reported losses. At the

---

[23] P. B. Musgrave, *United States Taxation of Foreign Investment Income: Issues and Arguments*, Harvard Law School, Cambridge, Mass., 1969, p. 28.

[24] From unpublished information of various government agencies of the Republic of Colombia.

[25] Individual company examples of effective return on net worth in the pharmaceutical industry:

| | | | | | |
|---|---|---|---|---|---|
| Case #1: | 197·3% | #6: | 38·1% | #11: | 88·8% |
| #2: | 94·4% | #7: | 402·3% | #12: | 256·8% |
| #3: | 247·0% | #8: | 126·1% | #13: | 56·5% |
| #4: | 708·3% | #9: | 44·2% | #14: | 378·9% |
| #5: | 962·1% | #10: | 138·0% | #15: | 352·8% |

same time, this subsidiary had price differentials of its intermediate product importations in comparison to 'international prices' amounting to 24·6 per cent of its net worth. The second wholly owned subsidiary in the electronics industry, for which data was available to us, declared in 1968 an 11·4 per cent return on net worth (including profit reinvestments). Yet the same company had a price differential on imported components from the parent corporation which amounted to a weighted average of 66 per cent. This could lead to an effective return on net worth from 50 per cent to 80 per cent depending on different assumptions about varying import policies.

Clearly the above figures still understate, sometimes quite considerably, the true rate of return to the parent corporations. Two reasons will be presented here. (a) Overpricing was calculated on the basis of comparison between FOB import prices in Colombia and FOB prices (sometimes list prices) reported in different markets around the world by distributors and manufacturers. For the parent corporation, particularly if it is a manufacturer, the internal list prices usually include considerable margins which cover fixed costs, profit allocations, etc. For example, research undertaken for the present work in the private sector in New England and the U.S. Tariff Commission in Washington, D.C., indicated that the margin of an electronics distributor could vary between 33 per cent and 50 per cent of the distributor's price.[26] Below this margin for the distributor lies the profit margin for the manufacturer, the margin to cover fixed marketing costs, the margin to cover fixed production costs of the manufacturer, etc. Since all these are fixed costs and profit margins, the 'international prices' taken to determine overpricing include further effective contribution to profits for the parent corporation. (b) To determine R. O. I. the denominator was taken as reported in net worth in the balance sheets of subsidiaries. Yet part of this net worth involves in some cases capitalization of know-how (which does not constitute financial investment at the subsidiary level for the parent corporation) and in several cases capitalization of machinery, new or second-hand (the price of

---

[26] For example: G.E. cartridge stereo VR-1000-3 was listed for $18·75 with a 33% distributor margin; G.E. cartridge stereo VR-1001-7 was listed for $11·31 with a 33% distributor's margin; Sonatone cartridge stereo 3T-S was listed for $5·84 with a 40% distributor's margin; Garrard Walnut base WB 1 was listed for $19·95 with a 50% distributor's margin.

which is generally determined by the parent corporation). For these reasons the denominator's value increases artificially and the effective return on investment (financial) is understated.[27]

2. A second major implication stemming from our analysis of collective inputs is related to the conclusion that certain returns to factors of production do not appear in the income determination of a certain activity since they are paid as part of the cost of other elements in the system, such as intermediate goods and services. Thus, the otherwise correct accounting procedure of measuring value added by excluding the cost of intermediate goods bought, to avoid double counting, hides in our case part of the returns accruing to the factors of know-how and capital. The true income-generating effects of a certain activity should account for the price differential between intermediate goods and capital assets on the one hand and their international price equivalents on the other. This additional monopolistic return to the transferrer of know-how and/or capital could possibly have important implications on measurements using the reported value added by accounting methods used at present.

For example, estimates of effective protection which compare tariffs with *reported* value added could significantly overestimate

[27] An example will serve our purpose on the matter. Let subsidiary A declare profits of $10 for its reported net worth of $100. In official publications then the R. O. I. will appear as 10%. Data presented in previous pages indicated that it is quite common in several manufacturing industries in Colombia to have an effective rate of return for the parent corporation of 50% as a result of overpricing which does not appear in official publications. Overpricing then will appear to be $40 in our example. The overpricing, though, hides further contributions to the parent corporation. Our empirical analysis in the electronics industry indicated that only the distributor's margin (which might have been included in our 'international' prices) varied between 30% and 50% of list price. This margin is in the range of figures of those of overpricing estimated for the Colombian electronics industry. To that one has to add all the relevant manufacturer's margins mentioned above. To keep things conservative, let us suppose that an equivalent of only 50% of the overpricing represented all these margins of distributors and manufacturers in the "international price'. For the parent corporation, though, these margins represent effective net contributions to profits. Hence our effective R.O.I. increases to

$$\frac{\$10 + \$40 + \$20}{100} = 70\%$$

If 20% of the denominator includes capitalized know-how and overpriced capitalized machinery, then the effective financial R. O. I. for subsidiary A is

$$\frac{\$10 + \$40 + \$20}{\$80} = 87.5\%$$

instead of 10% appearing in official publications.

such protection. A 'value-added' which includes the monopoly rents accruing to the foreign supplier of resources and which are transferred through the overpricing of intermediate products tied to these resources appears to be a more appropriate index of measurement. Also, estimates of efficiency of usage of domestic resources per unit of foreign exchange saved (in case of import substitution) or per unit of foreign exchange earned (in case of export promotion) could, as they are presently used, significantly overestimate the domestic costs *if* foreign exchange savings could be realized through appropriate pricing of intermediate imported products.

Another example arises in the case of estimation of the net income effects of foreign direct investments *to* the host countries. If intermediate product overpricing were considered as part of the effective value added accruing to the foreign resource transferrer, this could greatly affect income estimates. For example, for more than 40 per cent of the Colombian pharmaceutical sector the ratio of reported profits plus royalty payments to the domestic value added had a weighted average figure of 34·9 per cent. If, though, in addition to profits and royalties one includes intermediate product overpricing, then the weighted average ratio of income payments to the foreign investor divided by domestic value added was 152·8 per cent for 1968. In other words, for every dollar of income accruing to all domestic factors of production more than one dollar and a half accrued to the foreign investors who accounted for 40 per cent to 50 per cent of the whole Colombian pharmaceutical sector.[28]

[28] Company data:

| $\dfrac{\text{Profits + Royalties}}{\text{Domestic value added}} \times 100$ | $\dfrac{\text{Profits + Royalties + Overpricing}}{\text{Domestic value added}} \times 100$ |
|---|---|
| % | % |
| Case 1   13·4 | 90·0 |
| 2   23·2 | 124·5 |
| 3   4·5 | 106·0 |
| 4   34·8 | 229·0 |
| 5   30·2 | 47·6 |
| 6   91·7 | 314·0 |
| 7   36·4 | 150·0 |
| 8   17·7 | 44·8 |
| 9   126·5 | 323·0 |
| 10   32·9 | 277·0 |
| 11   29·0 | 144·0 |
| 12   83·0 | 112·0 |

# CHAPTER V

# Inter-industry Interpretation of Results

## A. EFFECTIVE PROFITABILITY OF FIRMS AND HOST COUNTRY GAINS

IN a given country, high effective profitability registered by foreign subsidiaries might reflect either or both of the following. It might be the result of competent management, superior technology, and availability of inputs (both local and foreign) at relatively low market prices.[1] Or high profitability could reflect the existence of monopoly rents which accrue (a) from tariff and non-tariff protection against foreign competition, (b) from practices that reduce domestic competition (such as domestic horizontal integration through acquisition of national firms or the use of scarce local factors such as bank loans creating availability problems to potential competitors), and (c), from legal and other protection against both foreign and local competition such as that resulting from patent laws. High profitability that stems from increased efficiency will imply, from the international point of view, gains through the reduction of resource costs resulting from such efficiency. From the national point of view, though, gains will take place only if the fruits of efficiency are shared partly by the host government through higher tax revenues from effective profits, or if local factors of production obtain higher returns than otherwise from the operations of foreign subsidiaries, or if efficiency is passed on to the consumers through lower prices.[2]

If utilization of installed capacity is one of the indicators of the degree of efficiency according to which firms operate, then in the Colombian pharmaceuticals, electronics, and chemical sectors such efficiency appeared to be quite low for national as well as foreign firms. This need not imply, though, a low managerial

---

[1] Cheap foreign inputs might result, for example, from the use of some services (like commercialization know-how) which the parent has developed, through investments in previous years, for which it does not charge the subsidiary.

[2] See H. G. Johnson, 'The Efficiency and Welfare Implications of the International Corporation', in C. Kindleberger (ed.), p. 55.

quality of the corresponding companies. Quite often it reflects a combination of small and segmented national markets coupled with rigidities in the technologies available. From interviews we undertook in the pharmaceuticals industry we found that most firms were operating at about 30 per cent to 40 per cent of one shift. In the electronics industry the corresponding percentage was around 45 per cent and in the chemical industry most firms were operating below 75 per cent of one shift. Since investment in equipment, buildings, and land account for about 50 per cent to 65 per cent of total uses of funds of subsidiaries in Latin America, the unit cost of under-utilized capacity might be quite considerable.[3] Capacity utilization did not indicate major differences between national and foreign firms within each family of products, although some joint ventures in the chemical industry showed the highest percentages of such utilization among all firms in the three industries.

The area, though, where foreign firms appeared to have an advantage over national ones was that of more specialized technology in the product groups of later vintage in each industry (e.g. synthetic fibres in chemicals and production of components in electronics). In terms of policy considerations the relevant question is whether such technology could have been obtained at a lower cost in the international market without necessarily being tied to foreign capital. It was only in the textiles sector, dominated almost completely by national firms located particularly in the area of Antioquia, that the percentages of capacity utilization reached 80 per cent or more of *three* shifts.

Low capacity utilization, other forms of production inefficiency as well as possible pressures exerted by foreign and national firms on government policies with respect to tariff protection resulted, in the late 1960s, in an arithmetic average of *ad valorem* tariffs for Colombia of more than 70 per cent for the major manufacturing sectors. (The equivalent protection for agriculture, fishing, and mining was 45 per cent, 52 per cent, and 20 per cent respectively.[4]) High tariffs as well as other forms of market protection and

---

[3] See 'Sources and Uses of Funds of Foreign Affiliates of U.S. Firms, 1967–68', in U.S. Department of Commerce, *Survey of Current Business*, Washington, D.C., Nov. 1970, p. 15.

[4] See Morawetz, 'Common External Tariff for the Andean Group', Economic Development Reports no. 209, The Center of International Affairs, Harvard University, Feb. 1972, p. 23.

concentration, rather than efficiency considerations, appear to be the major source of high effective profitability of foreign subsidiaries noted in the previous chapter. We pass now to consider the form of distribution or sharing of such profitability between host countries and foreign investors. For the former the channels through which income is shared are, as discussed earlier, fiscal earnings, payments to local factors of production, and/or lower than otherwise prices paid by the consumers.

In the countries in which we undertook research all foreign subsidiaries in the samples studied under-declared, sometimes considerably, the effective profitability accruing to their parent firms from their operations in such countries. Reported profits by foreign subsidiaries in Latin America are quite often much lower than those appearing in the rest of the world for affiliates of the same parents or lower than average profitability of local firms in comparable industrial activities in the host countries. For example, data from the U.S. Department of Commerce have indicated that the reported after-tax rate of return of U.S. subsidiaries in Latin America is lower than in the rest of the world, with the exception of Canada, for affiliates of U.S. parents in the manufacturing sector.[5] Similarly, work undertaken by the Colombian government indicated that the average rate of declared profitability as a percentage of net worth for foreign subsidiaries in the manufacturing and service sectors was 5·5 per cent in 1967 and 6·1 per cent for 1968. The corresponding figures for national, incorporated firms in the same sectors were 9·2 per cent and 9·3 per cent. Also the size of taxes paid by foreign subsidiaries normalized by the total investment undertaken by such firms in the manufacturing sector was about one-third of the equivalent figure paid by Colombian-owned incorporated firms in 1967.[6] The difference can be explained by the lower profits declared by foreign subsidiaries as well by their higher investment per firm which was utilized as a normalizing factor by the Colombian government in its estimates.

The above data do not prove that host government gains from

[5] See H. K. May, *The Contribution of U.S. Private Investment to Latin America's Growth*, The Council for Latin America, Inc., New York, 1970, p. 6.

[6] Source: Superintendencia Nacional de Sociedades, Division de Investigaciones Económicas, Anexo Estadístico 1971, as cited by the Departamento Nacional de Planeación in *Algunas Observaciones a la Política del País en relación a la Inversión Extranjera*, Documento DNP-978-UEIA, Bogotá, Sept. 9, 1971.

tax revenues on the profits resulting from increased efficiency or monopoly rents of foreign subsidiaries in developing countries are small. In some cases, particularly in the extractive sector, tax and royalty receipts for the host governments have been considerable, both in absolute amounts and relative to total government revenues.[7] Yet they indicate that in the manufacturing sector, at least in Latin America, government revenue rates from profit under-declaration by foreign subsidiaries are smaller than elsewhere both internationally and nationally. To the extent that some developing countries offer special tax incentives to induce investment by foreign companies, host government receipts are further reduced without this necessarily implying a net gain for the foreign companies which would have to pay taxes on profits remitted in other countries.

Fiscal revenues from the effective profitability of foreign subsidiaries are clearly not limited to corporate profit taxes. Host governments could obtain revenues from taxes on royalty remissions for know-how supplied by foreign subsidiaries. Generally, tax rates on royalty remissions are lower than corporate profit tax rates. Furthermore, fiscal revenues accrue to the host governments through tariff receipts on the imports of intermediates by foreign subsidiaries which use the pricing of such imports as a channel for effective profit remissions.

Given the empirical results we obtained on the different channels of effective profitability remission by foreign subsidiaries in the Andean Pact, it is possible that the gains of the host countries could be increased if policies were undertaken so as to promote a different distribution in the declaration of effective profitability. Such a different distribution need not always mean a net decrease in the global after-tax earnings of transnational enterprises. The host countries, though, could gain through higher national fiscal earnings. The net loss will accrue to another tax jurisdiction such as the home country of the parent. We will explore this further in the following section of this chapter on 'Channels of Effective Profitability Remission'.

A second gain that the country can obtain stems from higher returns paid to local factors of production. Many foreign investors

[7] In 1966, tax payments by all U.S. subsidiaries in Latin America constituted about 14·7% of the total fiscal revenues of the host governments. H. May, op. cit., p. 5.

are known for paying higher wages to domestic skilled workers than national firms do. For example. Chilean copper-miners who worked for U.S. subsidiaries in that sector were known to obtain a multiple (twice or more) of the average workers' salary and even more than that of miners working for smaller national firms. Similar cases were reported for bauxite-miners in the Caribbean islands. The same has not been so true for unskilled labour.[8] Higher payments to factors of production will result in net national gains for the host country if such payments are a result of higher productivity because of the foreign investors' contribution rather than because of monopoly rents or if such higher payments would not have accrued to other domestic factors of production in the absence of foreign investors. Otherwise such higher payments, for example to labour, will have income redistribution rather than net income gains for the host country.

With respect to the manufacturing sector, possible gains from higher payments to local labour will face certain limits in view of the relatively high capital intensive industries in which foreign subsidiaries usually concentrate in Latin America, excluding the indirect effects on employment resulting from such investment projects. This is not true, though, for countries like South Korea, Taiwan, etc., where several foreign companies invest in labour intensive processes such as parts of the electronics sector.

In Colombia, unpublished research undertaken in the National Planning Department indicated that out of 18 different industrial sectors, where foreign as well as national firms participated, 8 of them reported a net reduction of employment for at least three years during 1957–66, while investment increased in all of them during the same period. For the whole manufacturing sector in Colombia the amount of electric energy consumed (standing as a proxy for investment) per unit of labour employed increased between 1960 and 1967 by a factor of 1·5. Yet the industries where foreign subsidiaries concentrated indicate a corresponding increase much higher than the manufacturing sector average. For example, energy consumption per unit of labour employed increased by a factor of 2·7 in the chemical and pharmaceutical products, by 3·3 in machinery and electrical goods and by 3·7 in

[8] Our research in Colombia indicated that unskilled labour in the timber industry was paid, by foreign investors, wages very close to the country's legal minimum which in 1969 was 12 pesos per day. (U.S. $1 = pesos 19.)

rubber products during 1960-7.[9] Thus, unless wage increases to domestic labour more than compensate the limits on employment imposed by capital intensive projects, gains from the possible efficiency of foreign investments accruing to domestic factors of production should be sought in the returns to local capital, such as bank loans to foreign subsidiaries. To the extent that real interest rates of bank loans are often subsidized in developing countries,[10] it appears that lower, rather than higher, real returns accrue to such capital than the opportunity cost for the host country would have dictated under less imperfect capital markets.

We come now to discuss the relationship between foreign direct investments, the different forms of protection resulting from government policies against external competitive forces, and their implications for effective profitability. Table V. 1 presents the different tariff and non-tariff barriers of entry confronting imports of goods which could compete with those produced in Colombia by national or foreign firms in the families of products we studied.

## TABLE V. 1

| Industry | Imports prohibited totally | Imports permitted with prior government approval | _Ad valorem_ tariffs for permitted imports: | Prior deposits for permitted imports: |
|---|---|---|---|---|
|  |  |  | % | % |
| Rubber | All products |  |  |  |
| Pharmaceuticals | All products |  |  |  |
| Electronics | Some products | Some products | 100 | 130 |
| Chemicals |  |  | 30-40 | 30-70 |
| Textiles |  |  | 50-60 | 130 |

NOTE: Prior deposits represent the prepayment of the percentage appearing in the corresponding column on the value of imports involved. This can be translated to a tariff equivalent if the percentage of prior deposits is multiplied by the opportunity cost of money tied for each firm involved during the corresponding period between prepayment and actual importation.

For the products included in the prohibited list, market prices were partially controlled by a government agency after cost figures

[9] Data from the División de Recursos Humanos del Departamento Nacional de Planeación, as cited in _Algunas Observaciones a la Política del País con relación a la Inversión Extranjera_, DNP-798, Bogotá, 9 Sept., 1971, p. 17.
[10] See Alberto Musalem, 'Demanda por Dinero y Balanza de Pagos: La Experiencia de Columbia, 1950-1967' mim., Bogotá, Oct. 1970, Chapter I.

were presented by the firms concerned. Similar procedures were often followed for the establishment of tariff levels for the rest of the products by a different government agency. If Colombian market prices reflected the *ad valorem* tariffs, then the results of efficiency, if any, from local production were not passed on to the consumer. (This, as discussed on p. 66, was the third mechanism by which the host country could obtain direct gains from the establishment of efficient foreign subsidiaries.) The difference between CIF and FOB prices of products in our sample averaged between 20 per cent and 25 per cent while reported *ad valorem* tariffs were much higher.

The industry facing the potentially strongest price competition from imports was that of chemicals which could partly explain the relatively lower percentages of overpricing of intermediate product imports presented in Table IV. 3 on p. 47. From the three industries where final products were placed on the import prohibited list the pharmaceuticals and electronics appear to be those for which the highest protection could be offered for domestic production. This is so because the two industries, particularly the pharmaceuticals, have many real or apparent diversified products so that international price equivalents might be difficult to determine so as to aid the corresponding government agency in fixing upper price limits. However, the rubber industry in Colombia is basically oriented towards the production of tires for automobiles where product differentiation (quality or otherwise) with respect to international standards is not as high as in pharmaceuticals and electronics. This appears to be consistent with, and could partly explain, the inter-industry differences on overpricing we encountered.

The nominal (tariff) protection offered to Colombian national or foreign firms appears to be generally higher than any rate of effective profitability (expressed as a percentage of sales) which is within the range of our findings in the previous chapter. For example, a foreign subsidiary could be realizing 30 per cent of sales as effective profits. This could include 15 per cent from overpricing imports from its parent (if such imports account for 30 per cent of sales with a 100 per cent overpricing), 10 per cent of sales paid as royalties, commissions, etc., to the parent, and 5 per cent from declared profits of the subsidiary. Such an effective profit margin on sales is equivalent to about 43 per cent *ad valorem* tariffs confronting imports competing with the products of the foreign subsidiary. This 43 per cent is on the low side of *ad valorem* tariffs in Colombia, excluding other forms of protection. Thus the existing tariff structure compensated, in addition to profitability, for higher costs of goods and services bought locally, and for factors of production used in our hypothetical firm. However, since 30 per cent effective profit margin on sales is high (the average before-tax profit margin for the manufacturing sector in the United States was around 7 per cent in the late 1960s)[11] the obvious recommendation for government policy would be for some reduction in tariffs protecting products of foreign subsidiaries. The net direct gain for the country could presumably accrue to local consumers.

Yet such a recommendation, simple as it appears, overlooks the interdependence that exists between tariff levels or price structure in general and the presence of foreign subsidiaries within a country. A separation of existing tariffs, as an independent government policy, from the protected firms (national or foreign) is no more correct than, in analogy, the assumption that income growth can be treated separately from income distribution in a country. Tariff levels and quantitative restrictions are often set on the basis of direct pressures from the locally producing firms. For example, in the late 1960s the Colombian government attempted to reduce tariffs in the electronics industry. That policy was never carried through because of the reaction of existing national and foreign firms. Total prohibition of competitive imports was one of the conditions of entry negotiated by prospective investors in the primary petrochemical and synthetic fibre industries in Colombia. Also, indirect pressures on the setting of tariff levels are exerted by the presentation of costs by firms to government agencies concerned with fixing tariff levels. Such costs include the prices of goods purchased by foreign subsidiaries from their parents, the royalties charged, the interests accruing to inter-affiliate loans, together with the costs of local intermediate commodities and factors of production. Interviews in Colombia of top executives of foreign subsidiaries, regarding the low declared profitability of such firms, received as an answer the following: '. . . too good a profitability performance might give

---

[11] See *Business Week*, 'Third Quarterly Survey of Corporate Performance', 13 Nov. 1971, pp. 71–90.

the Colombian authorities ammunition to use against us particularly when companies request government authorization to increase prices.'[12] An appropriate policy on tariffs and other protection requires an understanding of and an appropriate policy on foreign direct investments and vice versa. In developing countries, like those of Latin America, where major parts of the industrial structure are controlled by foreign subsidiaries, governments cannot be assumed to pursue policies on foreign investments independent of tariffs, or on the latter independent of the former. The same is true for relevant fiscal and monetary policies which affect and are influenced by the presence or potential entry of foreign-controlled firms.

As far as domestic competitive conditions are concerned, in the Colombian market some concentration indices were provided in Chapter III. We proceed here briefly to discuss two causal factors that have an impact on this matter and, hence, on the effective profitability of foreign subsidiaries. The first refers to the mechanism by which foreign firms enter a host country. One such important mechanism of entry is represented by the direct displacement of national competitors through their acquisition. Data available on 51 U.S.-owned manufacturing subsidiaries that established themselves in Colombia between 1958 and 1967 indicated that 16 of them entered by acquiring existing firms.[13] In the chemical–pharmaceuticals sector the rate of acquisition was 42 per cent and in the food industry it was about 60 per cent. Detailed research on the matter in Central America[14] has indicated similarly high percentages on acquisitions of national firms as a mechanism of entry for foreign subsidiaries. Company analysis showed that quite often no significant changes in the rate of growth of sales and, various times, not even in product lines, were experienced after the take-over of national firms by the foreign companies.

Discussions related to the product cycle theory sometimes refer to the following general sequences of entry over time in different

[12] See *Business Latin America*, 6 Jan. 1972, p. 7.

[13] Data from J. W. Vaupel and J. P. Curhan, *The Making of International Enterprise*, Harvard Business School, Boston, Mass., 1969, as discussed by M. S. Wionczek in 'Hacia el Establecimiento de un Trato Común para la Inversión Extranjera en el Mercado Común Andino', *El Trimestre Económico*, vol. 37 (México, Apr.–June 1971).

[14] The research was headed by G. Rosenthal of the Secretariat of the Central American Common Market.

markets by technology holders, subject to some differences by size of firm, industry characteristics, etc.: during initial periods wholly owned subsidiaries are preferred, later, joint ventures are undertaken, and finally, when products are standardized and quite competitive, licensing arrangements are pursued with the late-comers. It is possible that in many sectors in developing countries quite often exactly the inverse sequence is followed by foreign technology and/or capital suppliers. Initially a licensing agreement with a national firm or simply a distribution franchise is arranged so as to develop both the market and knowledge about it by the licensor. Once the market is established possibilities arise for interesting the local government in some form of more intensive import substitution cum strong tariff protection. At that time the foreign company can enter by directly acquiring the local firm which previously distributed or put the last manufacturing touches on the corresponding products. The minutes of the Colombian Committee of Royalties indicated cases of attempts by foreign licensors to interrupt licensing contracts with the intention of entering into local manufacture of the products involved. The Committee's intervention prohibited the interruption of such contracts. Or a foreign firm can enter into a joint venture with a local concern and then progressively acquire majority or total control. We followed four such cases in Colombia, one in the glass industry, two in pharmaceuticals, and one in rubber. No cases were found where a joint venture became progressively a nationally owned firm.

The displacement of local firms through such high percentages of acquisition, as noted in Colombia, can accentuate monopolistic conditions in a market heavily protected against competition by imports. Thus, acquisition of national firms could explicitly appear in the selection of mechanism of entry by transnational corporations because of its monopoly-inducing effects. A different explanation has been suggested elsewhere which considers selection among mechanisms of entry principally on a relative cost basis for establishing activities in a country. In that sense it 'reflects nothing of the purpose for which that firm wishes to establish itself as a producer in a market (that is, whether its purpose is to complete, or to organize more effective monopoly arrangements)'.[15] Relative cost considerations certainly exist but,

[15] See H. G. Johnson, op. cit., p. 55.

in addition, there is no reason why monopoly-induced effect should not *a priori* be considered. Even if the costs of acquisition might be higher than a direct establishment (precisely because the local firm might share in its price part of the future monopoly rents of the purchaser), acquisition will still be preferred if the net present discounted value of monopoly rents exceeds that which will accrue under a different market structure in the presence of a local competitor for a given time.

Finally, we will consider some of the monopoly effects created by the patent system in specific industries that were included in our sample. The diversity of modern technology and its requirements with respect to requisite know-how have made the latter increasingly more important in creating particular company advantages and, in turn, have reduced the relative importance of the monopoly privileges extended through the patent system. Yet such a decrease in the relative importance of patents in creating monopoly power need not have always occurred in developing countries since the time-lag existing between product or process innovation and actual production makes possible the availability of alternative sources of supply for a given know-how. Yet, patents that cover such know-how, within the time of their duration, imply an exclusivity in terms of origin. However, the same time-lag could allow the development of alternative (patented) products and processes which are close substitutes.

Studies undertaken in the middle and late 1950s on patents and patent cross-licensing concluded that restrictive practices made possible by them 'appeared in enough critical industries that they must be counted as a significant factor in world trade'.[16] The cases identified were related, among others, to products such as acetic acid, activated alkalis, treatment of sulphur, various families of pharmaceuticals, latex and related synthetic rubber products, synthetic fibres and plastics, and a series of processes involved in mineral treatment.[17] These products are precisely those which during the 1960s, foreign subsidiaries in developing countries began to produce. Our research in the Andean Pact[18] indicated

[16] United States, Committee on the Judiciary, 'The International Patent System and Foreign Policy', 85th Congress, 1st Session, 1957, p. 10 (the study was prepared by R. Vernon).

[17] See, for example, Erwin Hexner, *International Cartels*, University of North Carolina Press, Chapel Hill, 1943, pp. 184 et seq.

[18] For more complete analysis on the subject see, C. V. Vaitsos, 'Patents Re-

hree major characteristics of patents in these countries. First, a progressive denationalization in the ownership of patents granted in such countries was noted. Table V. 2 depicts the case of Chile.

## TABLE V. 2

Year  Percentage of patents registered in Chile and owned by

|      | Nationals % | Foreigners % |
|------|-------------|--------------|
| 1937 | 34·5        | 65·5         |
| 1947 | 20·0        | 80·0         |
| 1958 | 11·0        | 89·0         |
| 1967 | 5·5         | 94·5         |

SOURCE: CORFO, 'La Propiedad Industrial en Chile y su Impacto en el Desarrollo Industrial', Santiago, Sept. 1970, p. 15.

Second, important concentrations in the ownership of patents were noted both by industry as well as by companies. For example, more than 40 per cent of the patents granted in Chile in 1967 were in the pharmaceutical and chemical industries while the second most important sector was that of mining and metallurgy with 12 per cent of the patents. In both cases more than 98 per cent of them were foreign-owned. Also in a sample of more than 2,500 patents in the pharmaceutical industry in Colombia more than 60 per cent of them were controlled by less than 10 per cent of all patent holders (all of them foreign). The same concentration indices were noted in a sample of about 1,000 patents in the synthetic fibre and basic chemicals industry. Third, the most important finding of our research was that the actual exploitation of patents in the Andean countries was extremely low. In Colombia out of a total of 3,513 patented processes and products examined (2,534 of which belonged to the pharmaceutical industry and the rest to textiles and chemicals) only 10 were actually produced in that country in 1970. In Peru, from a sample of 4,872 patents examined in such diverse sectors as electronics, food processing, pharmaceuticals, machinery and equipment, chemicals and metal processing, only 54 were reported as being exploited.

visited: Their Function in Developing Countries', *Journal of Development Studies*, vol. 9, no. 1 (Oct. 1972), and in Spanish, *El Trimestre Económico* (México, Jan. 1973).

Thus, patents granted by the Andean countries are not only almost in their totality foreign-owned but they are almost in their totality non-exploited. It is true that a large number of the products would not have been produced, or possibly even imported, by the Andean countries, even in the absence of patents, because of scale, technology, demand, and other reasons. Yet for other products the principal motive for undertaking, but not exploiting, patents was the consequence of company strategy with respect to two objectives. One of them referred to the possibility of securing monopoly position in import markets since existing patent legislation in the Andean Pact and generally around the world grants to the patent holder not only the privilege of exclusive production (which can be altered only through licensing), but also the privilege of exclusivity in importing and selling. Thus, patent holders can claim monopoly prices for the patented products when imported to a country.[19] The second objective, directly related to the above, refers to the possibility of extending exclusive monopoly privileges (stemming from the importation of intermediate products) for securing monopoly positions in forward linkages which use such imported inputs.

In the absence of adequate, or any, anti-monopoly legislation in developing countries to control such practices, monopolists of certain intermediate goods can become monoproducers in forward-linked productive activities. Such positions in the 'final' product markets enable the accrual of monopoly prices and rents in the importation of intermediates as discussed in the first objective above. For example, the patent holder of latex in Colombia or Chile, through the exclusivity in selling this synthetic rubber, can control which company will produce automobile tires using latex as an input. Similarly, patent holders in active substances can determine which companies can process them in the pharmaceutical or chemical sectors in countries such as those of the Andean Pact. Usually the subsidiary of the patent holder of an intermediate product becomes the monoproducer and monopolist

---

[19] For example in 1970 the German-owned firm that controlled the patent on indometacine sold that product to the Colombian Government for Col. pesos 770/thousands units. A North-American-owned firm without access to the patent offered the same product for Col. pesos 133·50/thousands units. The Colombian government was forced to buy from the German firm by a court decision based on the patent coverage. See *El Tiempo*, Bogotá, 2 June 1970.

of the related final one. In this manner monopoly privileges are extended into areas where patents do not exist.

In our industry samples in Colombia, pharmaceuticals were by far the most affected by existing patent legislation in that country. The concentration of production in that industry by families of products in one or few firms can be attributed, to a large extent, to the type of patent protection granted. Most of the licensing contracts on technology studied in pharmaceuticals included patents, and the product line of foreign subsidiaries matched the patent holdings of their patents. In direct interviews with Colombian national firms it was indicated that, in the absence of patents, they could produce close to 90 per cent of the products now under foreign control. Such production could be undertaken either with already developed or copied know-how or with the technical assistance of non-patent holders.

Among the five industries we studied, pharmaceuticals predominantly, and rubber secondarily, indicated industry-wide monopoly effects of the patents. The high profitability and overpricing of intermediates found in our analysis of pharmaceuticals could depend, to a large extent, on such monopoly effects of patents. Similar conclusions have been reached in studies undertaken elsewhere.[20] In the chemical and textile industries patent influence was related only to specific products (such as synthetic fibres) while in electronics it was practically *nil* given the early vintage of the products and their components assembled in Colombia.

## B. CHANNELS OF EFFECTIVE PROFITABILITY REMISSION

Given an effective profitability resulting from the over-all activities of a subsidiary in a host country, the parent can orient the remission of such profits through four basic channels.

1. Declared profits at the subsidiary level and remission through dividend declaration.

2. Interest payments on interaffiliate loans.

---

[20] The Till report, one of the main government documents presented during the Kefauver hearings in the U.S. Senate, gave evidence on the efforts of pharmaceutical firms '. . . to preserve the foundation of their prosperity, the patent system, by means of which they were able to control the market . . .', H. Harris, *The Real Voice*, The Macmillan Company, New York, 1964, p. 24.

3. Royalty payments or commissions for technology and other services.

4. Transfer-pricing mechanisms on interaffiliate sale of goods.

A rational selection among the different channels of effective profitability remission will depend on a constrained optimization policy whose objective function involves the maximization of the net after-tax cash flows available for the firm's global operations.[21] In a case where the coefficients (such as tax and tariff rates) that relate the channels of effective profitability remission to the maximization policy pursued are constant *and* such maximization policy is unconstrained (e.g. no upper or lower limits exist on pricing inputs) then one such channel could have been selected as the sole mechanism of remission. This, in turn, implies that a zero price would have been attached to the other goods and services exchanged between affiliates.

Yet the relationships involved are not always continuous and linear since, for example, corporate profit tax rates in some countries are progressive. Equally, constraints are imposed on corporate behaviour by government policies on the pricing of goods (e.g. as required by the U.S. Internal Revenue Service Code 482) or on the pricing of services (e.g. government negotiations on interaffiliate royalty and interest payments). There are two further reasons why only one channel of remission will not be selected. First, the effective profitability of an affiliate might not be given but it could depend on the channels themselves of its remission and the combination of their utilization. For example, the pricing of intermediate products imported from an affiliate could affect, as discussed earlier, the protection offered through tariffs and/or the permissible price charged in the host country for the goods produced locally. Thus, the channels of remission that increase effective profitability will tend to be preferred. Yet such channels might confront some upper or lower limits as well as non-constant costs. The second reason refers to the possible strategy of firms in diversifying, within certain cost considerations and other limits, the channels of effective profit remission so as to minimize the risk of any (future) government policy changing the relationship between effective profits and their remissions and hence affecting the

---

[21] A conceptual presentation of the elements of the maximization policy concerning the remission or use of the effective profitability resulting from the activities of a foreign subsidiary in a host country will be dealt with in the next chapter.

corporate net returns. Thus, most likely, firms will choose diverse channels of effective profitability remission taking into account the differential costs that each one of them implies. We proceed now to interpret the empirical results on remission of returns from the industry studies we undertook in Colombia.

### (1) *Declared profits and their remission*

The first and obvious consideration that arises in the case of declared profits is the tax rate that an affiliate confronts in its reported returns in the host country, as compared to the tax rate in an alternative fiscal jurisdiction where such profits can be remitted through other channels. Thus, if Colombian corporate tax rates were higher than in the countries where dividends of foreign subsidiaries are remitted, reported profits would, under certain conditions, tend to be under-declared so as to minimize over-all corporate tax payments. For most cases, though, the effective Colombian tax rate, including dividend remission taxes, is lower (being 45 per cent for a typical foreign firm) than the tax rates in the home countries of the parents where subsidiaries would remit their Colombian declared profits. Table V. 3 presents the percentage share of foreign direct investments in Colombia by origin.

TABLE V. 3

| Geographic Origin | Percentage of investments up to 1966. Total investments included U.S. $451 millions. | Percentage of investments during 1967–70. Total investments included U.S. $58 millions |
|---|---|---|
| | %₀ | % |
| U.S.A. | 68·7 | 55·7 |
| Europe | 16·7 | 25·4 |
| Panama, Curacao, and Bahamas | 11·4 | 10·3 |
| Others | 3·2 | 8·6 |

With the exception of Panama, Curacao, and the Bahamas, most investments in Colombia have an origin where parent firms confront a higher corporate tax rate than in Colombia (some exceptions exist in the case of Europe). So, in the presence of legislation that regulates double taxation issues, the tendency should have been, just on fiscal grounds, for firms to prefer profit declaration as a channel for remission since other channels could involve additional costs (such as tariffs on intermediate products imports or negotiations in the case of royalties). The data from Colombia, though, give evidence of exactly the opposite tendency. They indicate that firms prefer to declare as profits only a small part of their effective profitability.

One element that could explain the low rate of declared profits in Colombia is the ceiling of 14 per cent on capital invested that was imposed in 1967 as the top limit on profits that can be remitted abroad. For firms that utilize a large part of their Colombian-generated profits to finance, at least during some years, further expansion of their activities in that country, the 14 per cent ceiling might not be restrictive. In this way they could take advantage of the lower corporate tax rate in Colombia for reinvestments rather than undertake new capital inflows from funds taxed at higher rates. Yet for firms interested in remitting their profits abroad the 14 per cent will be equivalent for profits above that percentage, to a 100 per cent tax rate. They will therefore choose any other channel for such remission as long as such a channel will not imply an equivalent 100 per cent effective taxation as can happen with *ad valorem* tariffs above that rate in the case of transfer pricing.

The data from Colombia, though, do not show that the 14 per cent ceiling on remissions was reached by many firms in terms of their declared profitability. Information provided by the Balance of Payments Division of the Banco de la República indicated that the average percentage remission of profits with respect to foreign capital invested was 4·5 per cent for 1968, 4·8 per cent for 1969, and 5·4 per cent for 1970. These rates were lower than the interest payments on time deposits in Colombian banks, and lower than the prime rate for bank loans in the U.S.A. during the corresponding years. Out of 364 foreign companies which had undertaken 844 different investments in Colombia up to 1970 only 34 of them had reached the 14 per cent ceiling in their remissions.[22] The rest registered much lower percentages. Thus, if dividend remissions approximate after tax profit declaration,[23] a

---

[22] See Departamento Nacional de Planeación, *Algunas Observaciones . . . La Inversión Extrangera*, pp. 11–15.

[23] From 1960 to 1968, U.S. manufacturing subsidiaries in Latin America remitted

different distribution of effective profitability could have more than doubled profit tax earnings for the host government and still left foreign companies, on the average, below the 14 per cent ceiling. In terms of net fiscal effects, though, one has to subtract the reduction of earnings for the Colombian government which accrued from the other channels of effective profit remission.

Supportive evidence was encountered in Ecuador and Peru to the effect that transnational corporations might prefer to under-declare their effective profitability in certain countries, even if the corporate profit tax rates are lower than in the country where profits are remitted *and* even if no limits exist on profit remissions. (The case of Chile is not comparable since the tax rate for remitted dividends was 67 per cent for the years we had data on transfer pricing.) In Ecuador and Peru the relatively small samples examined on intermediates imported from affiliates by foreign subsidiaries indicated overpricing comparable to that encountered in Colombia. In the latter country, analysis of individual products for which data were available for 1966, when no limits on profit remission existed, indicated similar overpricing estimates as in 1969 when such limits were imposed. The following chapter will deal with the various factors that affect the relative size of declared profits as compared to the effective ones.

## (2) *Interest payments on interaffiliate loans*

This is a channel of effective profitability remission of considerable importance although it has not been incorporated and treated adequately in empirical analysis related to the foreign direct investment model. Data on Chile indicated that while the total foreign direct investment registered in that country between 1964 and 1968, originating from the U.S.A., West Germany, Switzerland, and the U.K., amounted to about U.S. $62,800,000, the total volume of foreign private loans coming from the same countries was about U.S. $174,871,000.[24] No exact estimate was provided of the percentage of these private loans utilized by foreign firms. Information from Colombia, though, indicated that

as dividends on the average close to 80% of their after tax profits. See P. B. Musgrave *United States Taxation of Foreign Investment Income*, Harvard Law School, International Tax Program, p. 31.

[24] Source: ODEPLAN, *El Capital Privado Extranjero en Chile en el Período* 1964–1968 *a Nivel Global y Sectorial*, Santiago, Aug. 1970.

about 60 per cent of all external private debt in 1970 was financing the activities of foreign subsidiaries.[25]

Interaffiliate loans for foreign subsidiaries in Chile could serve to avoid the high corporate tax rates, which are about 67 per cent, through interest payments, that confront a remission tax of 45·2 per cent. Similar reasons could prompt foreign debt rather than foreign equity financing with Chilean-owned firms, which otherwise, through debt capitalization, could have become joint ventures. The covenants of debt could possibly assure the control that participation in the ownership of the firm would have sought.

More precise figures in Colombia indicated that the debt/equity ratio of foreign firms was much higher than national firms. The average ratio of total assets to net worth for 1967 was 3·9 for foreign subsidiaries in the manufacturing and service sectors while it was 1·8 for national incorporated firms in the same activities. The corresponding figures for 1968 were 3·5 and 1·8 respectively.[26] As far as the relative importance of foreign private debt is concerned the following figures were noted: for every U.S. dollar invested in the equity of foreign subsidiaries, during the 1967–70 period, U.S. $2·1 were lent from abroad to the same firms. According to information provided by the Banco de la República, of the total foreign debt contracted by foreign subsidiaries in 1967–70 only 26 per cent was repaid by 1970.[27] Thus most of these loans represented long-term debt and for that part which corresponded to interaffiliate loans they could serve as a substitute to equity investment.

Interest payments on interaffiliate loans generally confront lower remission taxes than corporate profits and do not face (as often) limits on servicing remission or capital repatriation as profits and equity do. Furthermore, they do not imply additional costs such as tariffs in the case of transfer pricing on products. Finally, they are not as often subject to government intervention as royalty payments for technology and other services are. So they could represent an important channel of effective profit remission from countries which, through other controls, attempt to share

[25] See *Boletín Mensual de Estadística del DANE*, June 1971, p. 83.

[26] Departamento Nacional de Planeación, *Algunas Observaciones . . . La Inversión Extranjera*, part I, p. 7.

[27] Ibid., part II.

via corporate taxes part of the effective profitability accruing to foreign investors. The relationship of foreign private debt to equity investment in foreign subsidiaries in Colombia and the data from Chile presented above support such a conclusion.

### (3) Royalty payments

The use of information or technology by a company or person does not in itself reduce its availability, present or future. Thus, as in the case of public goods, the incremental cost in the use or sale of an already developed technology is close to zero for someone who already has access to that technology. In cases of minor adaptation (due to scale, taste, local condition differences, etc.) the firm incurs certain costs that it can estimate and which usually do not exceed a figure in tens of thousands of dollars. From the point of view of the prospective purchaser, though, the relevant incremental cost for developing the same type of alternative technology with his own technical capacity might amount to millions of dollars. Given market availabilities, the price between zero or tens of thousands of dollars, on the one hand, and millions of dollars, on the other, is determined solely on the basis of crude bargaining power. The range between the corresponding cost considerations is so wide that no price between them can be claimed to be more or less appropriate.[28]

The legislation applied in Colombia between 1967 and 1970, which covers the period of our data, considered royalty charges between affiliates as non-tax-deductible. Thus, negotiations on such royalty payments had purely a balance of payments objective and not a fiscal one. Foreign investors tried to remit royalties that were taxed as profits in the host country so as to avoid the 14 per cent ceiling on profit remissions. The government's negotiating objectives was the opposite. For the foreign investors royalty payments also served the purpose of increasing the reported costs upon which tariffs or price levels were negotiated even if for fiscal reasons they were counted as returns rather than as deductible charges. For all other countries in the Andean Pact

---

[28] For a discussion of the zero efficiency price of already developed technology, see H. Johnson, 'The Efficiency and Welfare Implications of the International Corporation', in C. P. Kindleberger (ed.). For the allocation of joint costs of planned, new R & D expenditures in the face of separate benefits see T. Horst, 'The Simple Analytics of Multi-national Firm Behavior', mim., Harvard University, June 1971.

royalties were tax-deductible and hence both fiscal and balance of payments considerations were involved. In a country like Chile with an effective tax rate on corporate profits of 67 per cent, which is higher than the equivalent rates in many capital-exporting countries, the fiscal effect of royalties was critical. Data on companies with a total of 399 contracts on technology which covered more than 80 per cent of the country's payment indicated that the ratio of royalty payments to declared profits was above 300 per cent.[29] This was much higher than the country average in other cases in the Andean Pact.

In Colombia the size of royalty payments in relation to declared profits by foreign subsidiaries in different industries was consistent with our analysis on effective profitability presented in the first part of this chapter. The industry which, as compared to all others, had an outstandingly high ratio of royalties to declared profits was that of pharmaceuticals. Foreign subsidiaries reported in the latter industry royalties that were on the average 400 per cent higher than their declared profits. In the rubber industry they were on the average 53 per cent. In the chemical industry, which had the lowest nominal tariff protection, most foreign firms in our sample reported a ratio of royalties to profits that was below 25 per cent.

In terms of ownership structure foreign firms in Colombia generally reported much higher absolute levels of royalties as compared to reported profits than national firms. For example, the royalties paid by foreign subsidiaries in the manufacturing sector were on the average 2·6 times higher per company than those of national firms in 1967 and 3·2 times in 1968.[30] Also analysis at the firm level indicated that in the rubber industry national firms paid the equivalent of 10 per cent of their reported profits as royalties while the equivalent figure for foreign subsidiaries was 53 per cent. Similar behaviour was observed in the chemical industry.

An interesting development was noted in the case of joint ventures which, in the few cases available, registered royalty payments which were higher than those reported for both wholly owned subsidiaries and national firms in Colombia. Such royalty payments generally accrued to the foreign equity holders in joint ventures. For such firms, profit declaration implies, obviously, a participation of national equity holders in dividends. For the foreign partners this is equivalent to a tax (whose rate is reflected by the national participation) and for which no equivalent tax credit is obtained in the home country as in the case of wholly owned subsidiary profit taxes paid in the host country. Thus, foreign shareholders will be interested in increasing royalty payments accruing to them and thus decreasing reported profits that have to be shared with the local participants. In the Colombian chemical industry, foreign subsidiaries, as mentioned above, reported royalties that generally amounted to less than 25 per cent of reported profits. Yet for joint ventures in the same industry the same ratio averaged 32·3 per cent for three firms and 142 per cent for three others. In two firms in the pharmaceutical industry royalties amounted to 7·5 per cent to 10 per cent of sales for know-how provided by the foreign equity participants with contracts lasting ten years. The same firms reported royalties of 1 per cent of sales to foreign non-equity participants with contracts that lasted only two years.

Before concluding our analysis on royalties, an important element needs to be mentioned which affects the demand for technology of receiving firms or countries. In the formulation of the demand for information, as in all other markets, a prospective buyer needs information about the properties of the item he intends to purchase so as to be able to make appropriate decisions. Yet, in the case of technology, what is needed is information about information which could effectively be one and the same thing. Thus, the prospective buyer is confronted with a structural weakness intrinsic to his position as purchaser with resulting imperfections in the corresponding market operations. Formal equilibrium analysis can often lead to tautological conclusions in the absence of 'definite statements about how knowledge is acquired and communicated'.[31]

---

[31] See F. A. von Hayek, 'Economics & Knowledge', *Economica* (Feb. 1937), p. 33. Also K. Arrow, 'Economic Welfare and the Allocation of Resources for Invention', in *The Rate and Direction of Inventive Activity: Economic & Social Factors*, National Bureau of Economic Research, Special Conference Series no. 13, Princeton University Press, Princeton, N.J., 1962. Also, 'Above all, how can prices channel information when the bids that create prices will almost certainly be wrong ones if

## (4) *Transfer pricing on interaffiliate sale of goods*

All of the above three mechanisms of effective profitability remission (dividends, interest payments and royalties) can be identified quite explicitly both in the income statements of companies as well as at the aggregate level of a country's national accounts. As such, specific policies or administrative actions can be introduced by a government so as to regulate the flow of income abroad through these channels. Developing countries with a policy on foreign direct investments try, in one way or another, to confront income flows through profits and royalty payments in particular and some, more recently, through interest payments. On the restrictive side, policies imply stated or negotiable top limits on profit repatriation or on royalty payments. However, as a presumed stimulus to foreign investment, policies could include tax exemptions and other forms of inducement or guarantee for realizing such returns. The area, though, of inter-country income flows, where data availability—research, as well as direct government policies—has been rather limited, concerns the pricing of raw materials, intermediate products, and capital goods sold among affiliates of transnational enterprises.

Evaluation of the import substitution strategy of developing countries has indicated their increasing dependence on such goods in their total import bill. A large percentage of these goods are imported by foreign subsidiaries from their affiliates. For example, research in the principal industries of the manufacturing sector in Colombia indicated that intermediate product imports by foreign subsidiaries amounted to 47·8 per cent of the country's total imports in these industries.[32] (Similarly, in the case of exports from subsidiaries of foreign companies in the Latin American manufacturing sector the percentage of such exports going to other affiliates is very high. In 1966, for example, sales to other foreign affiliates accounted for 52 per cent of the total exports of U.S. manufacturing subsidiaries from Latin American countries.[33]) Transfer

---

not based on the information bid for?', W. Paul Strassmann *Technological Change and Economic Development,* Cornell University Press, Ithaca, N.Y., pp. 25–6.

[32] See Departamento Nacional de Planeación, *Algunas Observaciones . . . la Inversion Extrangera* Part II.

[33] Data of the U.S. Department of Commerce as cited by H. K. May, *The Contribution of U.S. Private Investment to Latin Americas,* p. 38.

pricing on these inputs among affiliates results in implicit income flows whose detection is much more difficult than the explicit flows, and their control is equally more burdensome. Yet, precisely because of their implicit nature and the lack of direct disclosure of net income flows, transfer prices could constitute one of the most important channels of effective profitability remission. However, the pricing of imported products by foreign subsidiaries could imply costs for the receiving firm and hence for the consolidated accounts of the corporate system. These costs stem from the tariff rates and other indirect fiscal charges that confront imports. When such costs for the corporate system exceed those of the other mechanisms of remitting effective profitability, firms will tend to reduce the prices of goods imported from their affiliates and increase the flow of remission through other channels.

It is not surprising, then, that tariffs affecting intermediate products and capital goods, sold by a parent firm or its affiliates to a given foreign subsidiary, are singled out as one of the most important elements in negotiations with host governments. It is not so much that such tariff payments will reduce the competitiveness of the foreign subsidiary by increasing its costs. This, in the local market, could be corrected by passing additional costs to the consumer through final product tariff adjustments. It appears that the key factor in negotiating lower tariffs (or total tariff exemptions) rests on the restrictions they place on over-all corporate financial planning. Experience has shown in various cases in the Andean Pact that company negotiators attach a higher value to intermediate product tariffs than, for example, to limits on profit repatriation. The representative of a host government is most likely to accept such a negotiable element to increase the competitiveness of the foreign-owned local industry. This certainly appears necessary if possibilities of exports are promised. Yet in so doing, governments might be inducing the transfer of untaxed income from their countries abroad, while possibly increasing the competitiveness of the local industry. Increase of competitiveness, of course, will result only if lower tariffs do not induce the foreign parent or its affiliates to increase the price of goods sold to a subsidiary in the host country.

Our research in Colombia (see Table V. 4) indicated the percentage of imported intermediate products and raw materials in the total goods used by the companies included in the sample of five industries studied for 1968–9.

TABLE V. 4

| Ownership Structure | Pharma-ceuticals | Chemicals | Rubber | Textiles | Electronics |
|---|---|---|---|---|---|
| | % | % | % | % | % |
| Foreign-owned | 76·7 | 53 | 58 | — | 51 |
| Joint ventures | 70 | 55 | — | — | n.a. |
| Nationally owned | 56 | 77 | n.a. | 2·5 | n.a. |

In relative terms pharmaceuticals appear to be the industry with the greatest dependency on foreign imports. Thus, remittance of effective profitability through intermediate products over-pricing (after tariffs and top limits and taxes on profit, royalty and interest payments are considered) is potentially of higher significance in this industry in Colombia. Other industries do not fall very far behind with the exception of textiles where backward linkages and domestic availability of raw materials (such as cotton) have reduced to a minimum external dependence on imported inputs.

In terms of capital goods the highest external dependence appeared to be in process industries such as chemicals and rubber. For example, in the latter industry 40 per cent of a foreign firm's initial investment was accounted for by the capitalization of machinery sold by the parent to its subsidiary. In textiles some local firms have integrated backwards in the production of their own machinery or are importing from diverse sources of equip-ment manufacturers, while in other industries interaffiliate machinery sales is a common practice. In electronics, machinery imports appeared to be of comparatively lesser importance than in other industries since present Colombian production consists basically in the assembling of diverse components for individual final products. Thus, potential profitability remission through capital goods overpricing is of relatively more importance in the process industries, given the present state of capital goods production in Colombia.

The Colombian 1969 tariff structure confronting intermediate products in the industries studied was as follows:

| Pharmaceuticals | 1% |
| Chemicals | 25%–40% |
| Rubber | 10% |
| Textiles | 15%–35% |
| Electronics | 30%–50% |

The industry with the highest noted effective profitability (given total prohibition of final products imports and patent monopolies), and with the highest dependence on imported intermediate products, confronted also the lowest tariff rate (1 per cent) on imported intermediate products. These three factors ((a): effective profitability of foreign subsidiaries; (b): intermediate product dependence; and (c): intermediate product tariffs) could explain why the part of the Colombian pharmaceutical industry that is controlled by foreign firms showed in both relative and absolute terms the highest figures of overpricing of imported inputs. Such overpricing in the firms studied amounted to 6 times the royalties paid and 24 times their declared profits. National firms, though, presented overpricing that was less than 20 per cent of their reported profits. Such overpricing could be explained in terms of tie-in clauses in contracts of technology or patent licensing and as a mechanism of capital flight by national entrepreneurs. Thus, ownership of firms in this industry affected significantly the degree of overpricing reported. Rubber, the industry with the second lowest tariff on imported intermediate products (10 per cent), presented the second highest average figure of overpricing (40 per cent) as indicated in Table IV. 3 (p. 47). Again, ownership structure affected in this industry the degree of overpricing which for the national firms studied was zero.

In chemicals, the higher cost of remission through overpricing, the result of the relatively high tariffs on imported intermediates, coupled with the relatively lower protection on final products, could explain the relatively lower percentages of overpricing noted in this industry. The other industry, where the cost of remission of effective profits through overpricing of intermediates was high, was that of electronics. Yet, in that industry significant rates of overpricing were noted despite the input tariff charges. This can be explained by the following. In 1969 the Colombian electronics sector had no contracts of technology purchase since the technology used for assembling electronic components was relatively easy and known. Thus, foreign firms were not able to transmit part of their effective profitability through royalties. As such, overpricing of inter-mediates together with interest payments on interaffiliate loans were the only channels by which the 14 per cent ceiling on remitted dividends could be by-passed. Intermediate product tariffs of 30 per cent to 50 per cent resulted in a smaller leakage in profit remission for foreign corporations than the equivalent of 100 per cent effective taxation implied above the 14 per cent ceiling on dividends repatriation.

A second factor that distinguished the electronics industry from the others was the high overpricing noted in the imports of nationally owned firms. Besides the case of capital flight, such overpricing could be explained by the low knowledge of local entrepreneurs regarding availabilities in the international market. The latter is quite imperfect since in many cases components are still sold collectively in kits and an organized search is needed to determine and negotiate the individual purchase of components. The protection existing in the Colombian market, which in nominal terms was at least 100 per cent, could offer national producers a comfortable, satisfying profit level. Inefficiency in procurement might thus not have been very much felt.

We proceed now to recapitulate the principal conclusions of this chapter. The process of direct foreign investments and/or technology commercialization, in the developing countries studied, contained in itself the creation of monopoly conditions in the host economies. Hence the effective profitability of foreign investors reflects not only the possible returns from increased efficiency but also, and in some cases more importantly, the monopoly returns, accruing from such market conditions. With respect to external competition the entry of foreign investors in a country is often conditional either upon the complete prohibition of close substitutes or upon high tariff protection. Such protection covers not only higher local costs but also generates part of the monopoly rents accruing to foreign investors.

A first-best corrective policy could imply the reduction of effective protection granted to foreign investors. Such a policy was enforced through *collective* action by the five Andean countries, starting in December 1971, by reducing in the case of Colombia the average nominal tariffs from 70 per cent down to 43 per cent, in parts of the manufacturing sector over a period of years. As of now, this does not appear to have discouraged existing or new foreign investors from continuing or commencing activities in Colombia. For Peru the corresponding tariff reduction was from 90 per cent to 43 per cent and for Ecuador from 106 per cent to 43 per cent.[34] Previous efforts by the *individual* governments to reduce tariffs, in some cases, were not always successful because of the pressure applied by the protected nationally and foreign-owned firms.

Yet first-best solutions do not always exist. The presence itself of foreign subsidiaries in developing countries affects through negotiations, the protection offered to them, as tariffs affect the propensity of foreign investors to enter in a country. The bargaining power of individual countries in defining appropriate tariff levels in the presence of foreign investors might often not be sufficiently strong.[35] In any case, a proper analysis of effective protection in sectors dominated by foreign subsidiaries implies an understanding of the mechanisms and internal financial policies of such enterprises. Host developing countries often have a limited availability of knowledge with respect to the above. A proper tariff policy could require first, in the relevant sectors, a proper foreign investment policy.

With respect to locally produced substitutes, the entry of foreign subsidiaries through acquisition of national firms reduces potential internal competition and adds to the problems of infant industry in developing countries those of infant entrepreneurship. In addition, technological rigidities (which require few producers in small-size markets), legal restrictions (such as the patent system), and preferential use of scarce factors of production by foreign subsidiaries (such as local capital) add to the concentration of production and further reduce competitive forces. Such structural market imperfections require second-best policies, some of which imply certain restrictions in the operations of transnational corporations in developing countries.

To the imperfections of the markets of goods produced in a host developing country are added the imperfections in the input markets. These stem from the collective existence of various

[34] Morawetz, 'Common External Tariff for the Andean Group', p. 23.
[35] See Carlos F. Diaz Alejandro, 'Direct Foreign Investment in Latin America', p. 226.

factors of production and products in a package form that implies resource flows in a model of foreign direct cum indirect investment cum technology cum intermediate and capital goods. This form of sequential monopoly enables foreign investors to pursue a constrained maximization policy in the remission of their effective profitability through various channels of intercountry income flows. Each of these channels implies different types of leakages of returns from the corporate system. Their optimum combination for the firm depends on two general factors. First, it depends on indirect and direct government policies (such as tariffs, taxes, royalty negotiations, limits on profit remissions, etc.) which impose costs or constraints on company behaviour. Second, it depends on the ability of the firm through the exercise of its economic power and control to select the channels which imply the least costs for it. For example, the non-existence of technology contracts in the Colombian electronics industry implied that foreign investors in that industry had to select other channels for their effective profitability remission. In the pharmaceuticals industry, *par excellence*, the heavy dependence on intermediate product imports, protected by patents and confronted by low tariffs, implied that foreign firms used this as a major channel of remission. In the chemical and other process industries potentially heavy dependence of host countries on machinery and equipment could make this channel an important one for remissions. Finally, as in the case of the Colombian textiles industry, significant and efficient backward linkages realized in the host country reduced the possibilities of exercise of monopoly power by foreign resource suppliers, which in this case was restricted basically to imposition of export prohibitions.

A last point remains to be raised before closing this chapter. Analysis of import substitution in developing countries has often indicated important limitations as to the extent of possible backward linkages in various industries. Such limitations are mainly due to technologically imposed minimum-size limits, that exceed market availabilities in developing countries. In addition, they are due to some scarce know-how and skill requirements. However, the pursuit of industrialization by applying 'last touches' on final products[36] with a high dependence on trans-

[36] See A. O. Hirschman, 'The Political Economy of Import Substituting Industrialization in Latin America', pp. 8–9.

national corporations can potentially generate, as discussed above, other forms of inefficiencies for the host countries. Such inefficiencies stem, among other causes, from the effect that the lack of backward linkages could have on tariff and other protections of final products through the importation of overpriced collective inputs sold by foreign resource suppliers. In an imperfect economic world, industry analysis needs to be undertaken so as to determine which is the second-best solution. For example, the countries of the Andean Pact are planning the production of intermediate pharmaceutical products. Criticism has been raised by foreign firm representatives to the effect that the size of the Andean market will not permit efficient plant operations. Yet existing monopoly inefficiency, stemming partly from the effects of the lack of domestic backward linkages and realized through monopoly rents accruing to foreign input suppliers, could exceed production inefficiencies and thus amount to a third-best solution. Of course, there exists a fourth-best solution, if the Andean countries incur production inefficiencies and the foreign investors maintain their present monopoly rents through other means in the planned investment projects.

# CHAPTER VI

# Determinants of Transfer Pricing

In the present chapter we will deal with the causal factors and mechanisms that affect intercountry income distribution in the presence factors of vertically integrated companies operating across national boundaries. Such factors and mechanisms will include company needs (like preference on where a firm undertakes expenditure and investments) as well as company strategies (like those on technological ascendancy and pricing, interaffiliate debt–equity relations, etc.). Furthermore, we will relate some of the above company propensities (particularly those on location of major expenditures) to specific home and host government policies. The combined effect of company propensities and government policies will determine the resulting intercountry income distribution given the prevailing market imperfections.

As indicated in previous chapters the mechanisms of intercountry income flows in the foreign direct investment model include, in addition to profit remissions, the pricing of goods, technology, services, and credit among affiliates. We will use the term transfer pricing to indicate the corresponding prices for all such sales among affiliates without limiting it, as is often done, to the case of commodities.

Literature on transfer pricing of goods and services exchanged among affiliates of transnational enterprises generally treats the subject by taking into account the effects on such pricing of specific government policies of the countries concerned. This involves general government policies such as tax differentials among countries as well as tariff levels and other indirect fiscal charges on external trade. It also involves specific policies related to foreign direct investments, such as limits or negotiations on the level of profit remissions, royalty payments, etc. As such, transfer pricing and its impact on intercountry income distribution are viewed predominantly as a function of government policies and the effect that they have on company behaviour.[1] If one excludes policy-induced distortions of company behaviour that could result from limits on profit remissions or differences in income reporting techniques among countries, the issue of transfer pricing has been presented as amounting to a comparison between effective tax *differentials* on declared profits (including dividend remission taxes) and indirect fiscal charges, such as tariffs on the traded products among affiliates.[2] Since effective profit tax rates in different countries generally concentrate around the 50 per cent mark[3] and capital-exporting countries, like the U.S.A., give credit for taxes paid abroad, the conclusion is drawn that firms will minimize transfer prices so as to reduce the tariff payments of the importing affiliates.

The differences between the above conclusion on transfer pricing and our empirical findings presented in earlier chapters could be partly explained by the restriction on profit remissions imposed in Colombia after June 1967. However, for Peru and Ecuador, which had a lower tax rate than most capital-exporting countries and did not apply any restriction on remissions in the 1960s, the overpricing of intermediates in the presence of tariffs still remains unexplained with respect to the considerations mentioned above. We can generalize the case and ask why subsidiaries in countries with lower profit tax rates than those in the home country of their parents, and without any limits on

---

[1] For an analysis of the effects of optimum financial management due to differences in government policies and the advantage of centralized management in this area by transnational corporations, see S. Robbins and R. Stobaugh, *Money in the International Enterprise: A Study of Financial Policy*, Basic Books, New York, 1973.

[2] For a theoreticial presentation of the above see Thomas Horst, 'The Theory of the Multinational Firm: Optimal Behavior under Different Tariff and Tax Rates', *Journal of Political Economy*, vol. 79, no. 5 (Sept./Oct. 1971). pp. 1059–72. If $\tau_2$ is the tariff rate confronting imports by a firm from its foreign affiliates and $t_2$ and $t_1$ are, respectively, the effective profit tax rates in the host country of the firm and in the countries of its affiliates abroad, Horst derives the following conclusions: If $\tau_2 > [(t_2 - t_1)/(1 - t_2)]$, the corporation will be induced to minimize transfer prices in the pursuit of maximizing global after-tax profits. If $\tau_2 > [(t_2 - t_1)/(1 - t_2)]$, the corporation will maximize global after-tax profits by increasing, within possible limits, transfer prices. Ibid., p. 1061.

[3] See L. B. Krause and K. W. Dam, *Federal Tax Treatment of Foreign Income*, Brookings Inst., Washington, D.C., 1964. Some exceptions exist such as in the case of holding companies in developing countries and Western Hemisphere Trading Companies for which the effective tax of remitted profits in the U.S. is 36%. Also some fiscal exceptions exist in developed countries like the Japanese treatment on 70% tax exemption for royalty receipts, and Netherlands' treatment on foreign earned income.

profit remissions, should pay any royalties or have a non-zero price on intermediates imported from their parents.[4] Royalty payments could imply costs for negotiations, and positive prices on intermediates could result in tariff payments. The answer could partly depend on the scrutiny and diligence of the tax authorities in the technology and goods-exporting countries which might apply some rules on the minimum permissible price for inter-affiliate sales. In addition, the answer could depend, not only on such government policies, but on the financial, fiscal, and other managerial decisions of the transnational firms themselves. In other words, even if regulatory requirements did not exist and even if other relevant government policies were completely neutral (e.g. corporate taxes were the same among countries and tariff payments on goods imported were zero) corporations might still not be indifferent as to where they declare their returns. We will list the reasons for such an outcome immediately below and analyse them in the forthcoming pages of this chapter:

1. Given certain conditions, corporations will be induced, for fiscal reasons, to declare their returns in the countries where their affiliates have high expenditure requirements in comparison to the sales of such firms in their home markets and to non-affiliates abroad. We will call this the relative-expenditures-requirement.

2. Given certain conditions, corporations will be induced, for investment reasons, to declare their returns in the countries where they have the highest opportunity cost of money for company generated funds. We call this the relative-investment-requirement.

3. Over-all business strategy of the enterprise will also affect the selection of the countries where returns will most likely be reported. For example, transfer prices could influence the total *revenues* of the *paying* affiliates.

Given neutral government policies, the three reasons listed above affect transfer pricing as a result of specific company propensities or behaviour. As such, their effects differ from those generally appearing in the literature on the subject which take into account only the impact of government policies and their differences (e.g. tax differentials) on transfer pricing. We shall proceed to analyse these corporate originated effects on transfer pricing by assuming, first, neutral government policies. Later we

---

[4] This could apply to a country like Switzerland or to most Latin American countries in the late 1960s.

will introduce non-neutral government policies in order to evaluate the extent to which they can modify or, in some cases, reverse corporate behaviour. By neutral government policies we mean that:

1. effective profit tax rates are equal in all countries concerned as are income reporting techniques;

2. mechanisms exist for the complete avoidance of double taxation (e.g. credit is given for taxes paid abroad);

3. governments do not scrutinize the transfer pricing of companies;

4. indirect fiscal charges or costs are zero in the transfer pricing of imported goods (e.g. tariffs) or services (e.g. negotiations);

5. no limits exist on profit remission.

We will also assume at the beginning that:

6. local participants do not share equity in foreign affiliates (i.e. only wholly owned subsidiaries are involved).

## A. THE RELATIVE-EXPENDITURES-REQUIREMENT

Income earned from interaffiliate sales of goods and services by a firm is not necessarily declared as profit in its income statement. Rather it is included as part of the over-all receipts of the corporation as are sales in its home market or sales to non-affiliates abroad. Whether or not such earnings will result in the declaration of profits during a given year will depend on cost considerations of the firm and on the way it chooses to undertake and report expenditures or outlays as costs during that particular year, within the minimum reporting requirements set by fiscal agencies.

Given the ability of a firm to 'expense' certain outlays that are directed towards future returns (such as R & D) and given the capacity of a parent, through control, to define the degree of forward and backward linkage activities and hence, part of the costs of its subsidiaries, the parent (or some of its affiliates) declare in a fiscal year certain costs that are directed towards global operations over various periods of time. These costs include, for example, outlays for the production of components and intermediates to be further processed abroad. Or they include managerial expenses for global operations, R & D outlays, marketing costs, financial management, legal expenses, etc.

If these expenses, together with the direct costs for the

operations of a given firm, *exceed its revenues from sales in its home market and to non-affiliates abroad* (R), then it will be to the over-all advantage of the transnational enterprise to transfer untaxed income from its foreign affiliates through transfer pricing to cover these costs (C). In this way it reduces its global tax payments by reducing taxable income elsewhere through appropriate adjustments. It is important to note that under smaller transfer pricing the parent need not show losses since the difference between its revenues and costs could be more than covered by remitted profits after they have been taxed abroad. Thus, a firm's interests include not only the non-declaration of losses in any of its affiliates, but also the reduction of global tax payments through the coverage of the costs of each affiliate from its revenues (which include transfer pricing) *before profits are remitted from abroad.* Even if the parent firm declares losses (in the case where remitted profits from affiliates abroad are not sufficient to cover the difference between R and C) then, despite the opportunity to carry forward such losses for future tax savings, it will be to the advantage of the firm not to declare (or to reduce) losses in the home country by reducing taxable profits abroad through appropriate transfer prices. This is so since the corresponding future tax savings in the home country, through the carry-forward, will constitute only a percentage (namely the tax rate) of the taxes paid abroad for the declared profits of the subsidiaries during the previous years. Thus, only a part of the taxes paid in the host countries will be recovered through future tax savings in the home country if the parent declares losses.[5]

Thus, if $R - C < 0$, whether or not remitted profits from affiliates are sufficiently large so as to have profits being declared in the income statement of the parent, it will be to the advantage of the latter to increase the transfer prices of the goods or services sold to its affiliates (or reduce the prices of such inputs bought from them) so as to reduce their taxable income. The above can be seen from the following:

Let R and C stand as defined above. Also let $Y$ = additional income of a transnational enterprise to be allocated either as

---

[5] I am grateful to Mr. Paul Streeten for bringing to my attention the need to enhance my analysis by introducing the carry-forward repercussions. Yet, the latter do not alter the basis of the conclusions concerning transfer pricing if $R - C < 0$ as discussed above.

epatriable taxable *profit* at the level of the foreign subsidiaries
(Case A), or as income accruing to the parent through interaffiliate charges (Case B), and let $t$ = profit tax rate in home and
host countries.

Also assume that the revenues of the parent from sales in its
home market and to non-affiliates abroad are smaller than its
incurred costs. Hence $R - C < o$.

Then, the net *after*-tax profits of the parent from Case A ($P_A$)
after foreign earned profits are remitted, will be:

$$P_A = R + (1 - t)Y - C$$

No additional taxes will be paid in the home country since all
declared profits, after dividend remission from abroad, have
already been taxed in the host countries of the subsidiaries.

If $P_A > o$ then, the choice between Case A and Case B will
depend on the comparison between $P_A$ and $P_B$, where $P_B$ stands
for the after-tax profits of the parent from Case B.

$$P_B = (1 - t)(R + Y - C) \text{ if } P_B > o.$$

Hence, optimum company policy with respect to transfer
pricing will depend on whether:

$$P_A = R + (1 - t)Y - C \gtreqless P_B = (1 - t)(R + Y - C)$$

or, by simplifying, it will depend on whether

$$R - C \gtreqless (1 - t)(R - C)$$

since $R - C < o$; then $P_A < P_B$. Thus, positive transfer
pricing will be pursued up to the point where

$$R + (1 - x)Y = C$$

where $(1 - x)$ stands for the percentage of $Y$ that is remitted
through interaffiliate charges and for which no taxes are paid
anywhere, while $x$ stands for the percentage of $Y$ for which
taxes are paid in the host or home countries. After the parent has
covered its own expenses from income earned abroad, the
enterprise will be indifferent as to whether it remits income
through dividends or through transfer pricing, given our assumptions on neutrality of government policies. (For the proof of the
same conclusion even under carried forward losses for future tax
savings in the case where $P_A < o$ see Appendix 2.)

Interaffiliate charges could, thus, become an important element for optimum corporate policies. Such charges could not only cover the incremental cost of goods and services exchanged among affiliates but also pay part of the fixed expenses of an enterprise directed towards its global operations. These expenses can be called fixed in the strict sense that they do not (or need not) vary with the number of units produced during a given year. Yet, they are variable in the much broader sense according to which the use of resources by firms is conditioned by the availability of funds (or income in general) from global operations.

From the point of view of the host countries, the above considerations raise the question as to how far a particular economy should participate in covering the expenses undertaken by a transnational enterprise for the production of inputs (such as technology, managerial capacities, etc.) from which it, as well as the rest of the world, will profit. From the cosmopolitan point of view the same question can be put as follows: how should the world share in financing its overhead? If the world overhead generated by transnational enterprises, is highly concentrated in particular nations, other countries, although benefiting from it may come to question it and bargain in their payments for it. For example, in the case of U.S. corporations it has been estimated that they spend abroad, on R & D, only about 2·6 per cent of the total allocations in industrial research reported for that country, while 97·4 per cent is spent in the U.S. Furthermore, the R & D expenditures undertaken in the rest of the world by U.S. transnational enterprises are highly concentrated in terms of sectors (60 per cent was spent by the automobile and other transportation equipment sectors) as well as by countries (mostly in Western Europe and Canada).[6] Similar high concentrations, even ethnocentric preferences, exist for the case of top management posts related with the global direction of multinational enterprises.[7] Equally, despite some organizational, geographic, or other decentralization characterizing certain dynamic transnational

[6] See McGraw-Hill, 'Survey of Business Plans for Research & Development Expenditures, 1967–70', May 1967. For further discussion see K. Pavitt, 'The Multinational Enterprise and the Transfer of Technology in J. H. Dunning (ed.), pp. 74–9.

[7] See K. Simmonds, 'Multinational? Well not Quite', Columbia Journal of World Business, New York (Fall 1966). Also for further discussion see L. G. Franko, 'Who Manages the Multinational Enterprise?' mim., Centre d'Études Industrielles, Geneva, Jan. 1973.

firms, various basic overhead allocations are realized at the home office. Such activities involve central company planning, financial management, research on industry trends, legal strategy and protection, lobbying, etc.[8] To cover these basic expenditures which are absolutely necessary for the successful survival of the world-wide activities of an enterprise over time, a firm will have a propensity to reduce its profit declaration at the level of a foreign subsidiary and to increase the revenues earned by the parent. Such increased income can in turn be used to finance the above-cited expenditures in the home country.[8a]

Returning to our analysis of the firm and optimum transfer-pricing policy, we can estimate the additional funds (and hence resources) that accrue to the transnational corporation by increasing interaffiliate charges on the corporate units that have comparatively lesser expenditure requirements. Let $Y$, $t$, $x$ stand as defined earlier. Thus:

Additional funds available to the corporation from its foreign operations in Case A which implies no transfer pricing: $Y(1 - t)$

Additional funds available to the corporation from its foreign operations in Case B which includes transfer pricing: $Y(1 - tx)$.

Hence for all cases where $x < 100$ per cent it follows that funds generated in Case B > those from Case A.[8b] The difference between $Y(1 - tx)$ and $Y(1 - t)$ represents the difference of after-tax profits for the parent in the two cases. This also equals the difference of global tax payments for the corporation in the two cases. It is only when $x = 100$ per cent., that is when all foreign earned income is declared as profit by the parent, or its affiliates, that the two cases will be equivalent. This is the case

[8] The above consideration raises important questions about the economic meaning of the accounting definition of 'business savings' which involve reinvested profits. Other investments by the firm are reported as expenses (like R & D) due to prevailing fiscal policies. Such investments might far outweigh reinvested profits. For example the average reported retained earnings (excluding reserves) for the manufacturing sector of the U.S. in the late 1960s were below 2% of sales. Some sectors, like the pharmaceuticals, spent just on R & D about 6% of sales.

[8a] Similar problems have been noted with respect to state income taxes paid by corporations in the U.S. Distribution of income for the different States in the U.S. is settled on the basis of some crude formulas on sales and employment.

[8b] For a numerical example see Appendix 3.

when the revenues of the parent generated from sales in its home market and to non-affiliates abroad cover all the costs it incurs for domestic and foreign activities, directed towards present and future returns.

Thus, the more a firm depends on foreign earned income through subsidiaries (the more, that is, it becomes a transnational firm) *and* the more it tends to concentrate certain fixed expenses in one country, the more likely it is that *untaxed* income will be transferred by foreign affiliates to that country. The size of the domestic market where a firm operates and its exports to non-affiliates relative to the costs it assumes for its global performance become, hence, a critical element of how such a firm distributes returns among its affiliates operating in various countries. These countries, in turn, obtain not only different returns to factors of production but also have different tax claims depending on the strategy followed by transnational firms. A firm like Philips International, given its declared fixed costs, the tax rates around the world, and exports to non-affiliates, will have a higher propensity than, let us say, General Electric Co., to transfer income from its subsidiaries to the parent firm since the Dutch market is smaller than that of the U.S.

To the extent that many developed countries have parent corporations residing within their national boundaries, intercountry income effects, from the activities of various enterprises, can to a certain degree offset each other. A similar conclusion, though, cannot be drawn for developing countries. However, since the income earned from each one of these countries by foreign firms will most likely represent a relatively small part of corporate revenues, such income could have been declared, in any case, as profit by the parent rather than being used to cover its expenses. Hence, smaller countries could negotiate with foreign corporations a different intercountry distribution of the income generated from their markets, *if* appropriate policies were undertaken by them in this respect. Such a different intercountry income distribution could leave transnational enterprises in the same after-tax position as before. Yet, for the host countries, the additional tax gains could prove to be an important part of their total direct benefits from the operations of foreign subsidiaries given the possible low labour intensity of such firms and small over-all returns to domestic factors of production. Nevertheless, transnational enterprises might be reluctant to have different transfer prices for different countries since such policies could prompt pressures or even sanctions from fiscal authorities and other interested parties in the countries where lower taxable income is declared.[8c]

An obvious question still remains to be answered regarding how often transnational enterprises confront a situation where their foreign earned income is needed to cover part of the cost incurred by the parent firm. Companies guard, tenaciously, information related to the above question. No published data exist that could give us an adequate answer to this question. Yet, a clue can be obtained in an indirect way that suggests that the above condition $(R < C)$ is not an uncommon one for U.S. parent firms. For other enterprises, whose parent firm's home market is generally much smaller than that of the U.S., the occurrence of the above-stated condition will be even more common. A study published in 1966[9] indicated that out of 93 corporations, which figured among the list of the largest U.S.-owned transnational firms, 51 had a foreign content in their global sales that varied between 20 per cent and 49 per cent.[10] Sales, that is, of subsidiaries located outside the U.S. market amounted to something between one-fifth and one-half of the global (consolidated) sales of such enterprises. The higher growth rates of sales experienced by many subsidiaries in their host markets, as compared to the U.S., since 1966 would certainly increase the above percentages of foreign content in the consolidated sales figure.

Taking, then, as a hypothetical example, an enterprise for which its foreign-located subsidiaries account for one-third of its global sales, the following case can be depicted. Let the parent firm charge its subsidiaries the equivalent of 20 per cent of *their* sales for the following purposes: royalties on technology, fees for managerial advice, charges for other headquarter services such as legal and administrative services, royalties on trade-marks and

---

[8c] For the fear of the 'domino effect' on government action due to different prices charged for different final products in different countries see 'The Lords Reject New Inquiry on Swiss Drugs', *The Times*, London, 23 June 1973, p. 1.

[9] Data presented by N. K. Bruck and F. A. Lees in 'Foreign Content of U.S. Corporate Activities', *Financial Analyst's Journal* (Sept.–Oct. 1966), pp. 1–6, as cited by R. Vernon in *Sovereignty at Bay: The Multinational Spread of U.S. Enterprises*, Basic Books, New York, 1971, p. 122.

[10] The definition of foreign content varies from firm to firm since some include cases of exports from U.S.-located companies as part of local sales and others do not. The figures should obviously be taken in approximate terms.

other marketing intangibles, differences between prices and incre
mental costs of producing intermediate products and capita
goods sold to the subsidiaries, interest charges on interaffiliat
debt, commissions for exports of and/or imports by the sub
sidiaries that are handled by the parent, etc. Such charges impl
that an equivalent of 6·6 per cent of the *consolidated* sales represen
earnings registered by the parent from interaffiliate payment
charged to the subsidiaries. In terms of the parent's accounts, th
ratio of earnings before taxes contributed by the subsidiarie
to the sales *registered by the parent* (not the consolidated sales) wil
be equivalent to 10 per cent (6·6 per cent compared to 66 pe
cent). However, the average ratio of earnings after taxes to tota
sales registered by the whole U.S. manufacturing sector in th
late 1960s was below 4 per cent and close to about 3·8 pe
cent.[11] In before-tax terms this will bring the ratio to 7·3 pe
cent.

Thus, in our example, the net before-tax contributions to th
parent's earnings through charges to its subsidiaries exceed th
average ratio of earnings before taxes registered in the late 1960
by the whole U.S. manufacturing sector, all figures counted ir
percentage terms of the parent's sales (about 10 per cent versu
7·3 per cent). In other words, under plausible assumptions or
interaffiliate charges, we found that sales to the domestic marke
(or to non-affiliates abroad), for our hypothetical firm, were no
enough to cover the costs incurred by the parent for its *globa*
needs using as a base the actual figures reported on the matter
for the U.S. manufacturing sector. Hence, in our example, ne
earnings contributed by foreign subsidiaries covered not only al
of the profits reported by the parent but also part of the costs
undertaken by the parent. The plausibility of the assumptions
used in our hypothetical example, combined with the actua
profitability figures for the U.S. manufacturing sector, leads us to
conclude that the case described is not an unlikely one. It could
describe the possible situation confronting various transnational

[11] See, for example, *Business Week*, 'Third Quarterly Survey of Corporate Performance', 13 Nov. 1971, pp. 71–90. Various transnational enterprises have not only
higher growth rates on sales but also higher profit ratios than the sector averages.
Thus the 3·8% will be an underestimate of their returns. Yet the figures presented
above did not include the remitted declared profits of the subsidiaries. These remissions could account for most of the difference between profit ratios of transnational
enterprises and sector averages.

nterprises. The non-publication by firms of more precise data makes this indirect way of reaching our conclusion the only possible means of analysis.

## 3. THE RELATIVE-INVESTMENT-REQUIREMENT

Intercountry income distribution will tend to be affected not only by the issues on relative *expenditures* or costs raised above, but also by the relative-*investment*-requirements that confront a firm in its transnational operations, as far as these can be financed by company-generated funds. Differences in the opportunity cost of capital among different countries will tend to affect a firm's propensity as to where it chooses to declare its earnings for further use by the firm.

Such considerations are applicable when various standard government regulatory requirements are introduced to the foreign investment model. For example, remitted profits from abroad might be receivable only after the end of the fiscal year and after such remittances have been cleared by the tax authorities and, possibly, by the foreign exchange authorities of the host countries. However, income can be transferred *continuously* during the year, and at the choice of the parent, through interaffiliate charges. The funds generated by sales to affiliates, registered through interaffiliate transfer pricing, can be used for the investment plans of the corporations. Two factors enter here in the management of company-originated sources of funds. First, the time element mentioned above, which allows a fluidity of funds for appropriate use by sales to affiliates while remitted earnings are generally constrained to a period after the end of the fiscal year. Second, during the relevant time, funds are available for use untaxed, while reinvested profits remitted from abroad imply a forgone availability of funds through prior payment of taxes.

The most obvious case where these factors apply is that of countries that confront *continuous* inflation and *periodic* adjustments in their exchange rates to correct their overvalued currencies. The opportunity cost of funds tied up in a country, until they can be remitted abroad as profits for further use by the corporation at the end of the fiscal period, can be reflected by the forgone increase in the firm's net returns by earlier remittances, through transfer pricing, before devaluation corrects inflation-caused imbalances. Thus, although long-run trends of devaluation and inflation of the currency of a country could offset each other corporate policies in the short run, through optimum transfer pricing on interaffiliate charges, can maximize global after-tax returns. Host countries will forgo not only taxes on returns resulting from possible increased efficiency generated by the activities of transnational enterprises, but in addition they will forgo taxes on inflation-generated returns. The countries which will more likely confront such situations are the developing ones with their history of inflation and devaluation cycles.

In the more general case, higher opportunity cost for company-generated funds in country $x$ than in country $y$ can be met directly, through interaffiliate charges, rather than periodically at the end of each fiscal year through profit remittances. Such occurrences become particularly important once controls on capital flows are introduced to the system.[12] For example, in the 1960s the U.S. government constrained, by various means, capital outflows for direct investments of U.S. corporations in Europe. In the face of such controls, companies could have been prompted to underprice goods and services sold by the U.S. parents to their European affiliates. In this way they could have implicitly achieved capital outflows whose explicit realization was limited through governmental policies.[13]

Both the relative-expenditures-requirement and the relative-investment-requirement indicate that, even in the absence of profit tax differentials among countries (and assuming for this section no costs on transfer pricing), firms are not indifferent as to where they declare their returns. Global after-tax profits can be maximized through profit minimization in certain countries with corresponding intercountry income distribution effects.

---

[12] For the use of a generalized networks systems approach to direct corporate behaviour in view of the IRC Subpart F regulations of the U.S. 1962 Revenue Act and the 1968 regulations of the Office of Foreign Direct Investment of the U.S. government, see D. P. Rutenberg, 'Maneuvering Liquid Assets in a Multinational Company: Formulation and Deterministic Solution procedures', *Management Science*, vol. 16, no. 10 (June 1970), pp. B-671 to B-684.

[13] The U.S. government used the Internal Revenue Service Section 492 to prosecute companies in the oil industry which undertook such practices during that period. For a court decision in another industry see 'Eli Lily & Company versus The United States' 372 F.2d 990, 178 Court of Claims (no. 293–61, Decided 17 Feb. 1967), pp. 666–733.

## C. OVER-ALL BUSINESS STRATEGY AND TRANSFER PRICING

### (1) *Transfer pricing and revenues of affiliates*

We will discuss three specific cases of the effect that inter-affiliate charges could have on the revenues (rather than simply on profits) of the firms concerned and the impact that this has for global after-tax profits of the transnational enterprise.

First, as discussed in the empirical analysis of previous chapters, interaffiliate charges can affect the revenues of the *paying* firm, through the impact that such charges can have on tariff protection offered by the host governments on goods produced domestically. This can increase the global after-tax profits of the transnational enterprise even if it reduces the profits of the particular affiliate. If transfer pricing is costless then interaffiliate charges will be increased up to the point that the subsidiary's effective returns will be maximized through higher tariffs on the final goods produced. However, higher tariffs could induce potential competitors to undertake import substitution of such products with corresponding risks for a transnational enterprise both at the final and intermediate product markets. If transfer pricing is not costless then corporate behaviour, in addition to the above considerations, will depend on the comparison between increased revenues from final product tariffs and increased costs from tariffs on intermediates, given constant production costs.

Second, interaffiliate charges can affect the subsidiaries' revenues and this, in turn, can affect the parent's tax liabilities as in the case of depletion allowance in the petroleum industry. In such a case, transfer pricing of exports *from* the subsidiary will be increased and this, *ceteris paribus*, will increase both the before- and after-tax profits of the subsidiary and the after-tax profits of its parent. Such a policy will be pursued as long as additional host country claims, or potential claims induced in the future by present profitability performance, do not exceed the tax savings of the parent resulting from the increased revenue of the subsidiary.

Third, interaffiliate charges, by affecting the liquidity of subsidiaries through changes in cash revenues, can affect a particular firm's access to non-company funds, such as bank loans. This will depend on the prior liquidity requirements of each subsidiary and the effects of additional liquidity on new external funds. Furthermore, it will depend on the standards of lenders in judging each subsidiary as an independent firm or as financially covered by the transnational enterprise itself.

### (2) *Technological ascendancy, other forms of monopoly power and reporting of returns*

The technological ascendancy that a vertically integrated firm enjoys in particular processes or products can affect where it chooses to declare its profits. Such enterprises probably prefer to declare their returns, not only at the place where future expenditures or investments are needed, but also at the level where they have a technological advantage over their competitors. They can, thus, underprice the latter in markets of easily acquired technology if market prices are influenced by the transfer pricing of the technology leaders. For example, if the distribution of petroleum presents no major know-how problem, oil companies might choose to operate at a loss at the distribution level in order to underprice competitors, while obtaining their profits at another level or country where they might control processing technology. In the gas industry, cryogenic technology in transportation and distribution might lead companies to declare profits at those levels while operating at a 'loss' at the level of extraction. In the automotive industry the 'deletion allowance' in pricing 'completely knock down' (CKD) parts can bring about, among other effects, the inhibition of new entrants in certain parts of component production.[14]

Similarly, other forms of monopoly, such as patent holdings, can be used to affect profit declaration at different levels by transnational enterprises with direct effects on income distribution among countries. For example, ownership of oil pipes and monopoly of transport has proven in the past to be a key element in the cartelization of the petroleum industry.

### (3) *Profitability and political considerations*

Developed countries (like Canada, and, in the early 1960s, France) and almost all developing countries have translated the

---

[14] Negative effects on domestic components suppliers in the automotive industry that resulted from the 'deletion allowance' practices of foreign subsidiaries have been discussed by S. Kleu in 'Import Substitution in the South African Automobile Industry', unpublished doctoral dissertation, Harvard Business School, 1967.

varying degrees of domination of their industries by foreign transnational firms into very explicit political considerations. Practically no major Latin American political movement or party exists which does not consider as one of the pillars of its platform the issue of foreign direct investment. Nationalist positions (whether by 'right' or 'left'-leaning political parties), if translated into concrete economic policies can endanger, to some degree, the interests of transnational enterprises in certain markets.[15]

Clearly, from the economic and political point of view, the major cause of preoccupation stemming from a country's industry domination by foreign subsidiaries is the complex issue of control. Yet the most easily identifiable element, at least for political pronouncements, is that of profitability of foreign subsidiaries. This, in turn, can be translated into statements of balance of payments and income costs or within the broader aspects of 'exploitation models'. Notions related to the determination of market shares, foreign participation, and repercussions from loss of control are often too subtle to express or interpret. Percentages of rate of return (particularly that which is declared) constitute, on the other hand, a much more palatable political medium of expression. Thus transnational enterprises might follow a policy of under-declaring the returns of their subsidiaries in certain markets (particularly those of developing countries), even if this might occasionally run contrary to their tax, tariff, and other interests, as a protective move for their long-run interests and acceptance in certain markets.[16]

---

[15] The reactions and pressures of the representatives of transnational corporations against the recent Andean Pact Code on foreign investments is a well-documented case. See M. S. Wionczek, 'La Reacción Norteamericana ante el Trato Común a los Capitales Extranjeros en el Grupo Andino', *Comercio Exterior*, 6 May 1971. Also the decision of the Argentinian ex-minister of Economy, Aldo Ferrer, to direct government purchases to goods and services produced by Argentinian-owned firms has created strong reaction by foreign firms. (Governments of developed countries have long practised similar nationalist policies.)

[16] Referring to a comment in a radio broadcast from Panama on the magnitude of profits of U.S. investments, a study undertaken by the RAND Corporation concluded the following: 'If we seek to promote U.S. investments in Latin America in the future as a means of furthering U.S. national interests, it is not enough that *we* believe the investment works for the material benefit of the host countries. Quite regardless of how much objective truth is on our side, the position of the United States will suffer if the antagonists kindle anti-American sentiments by successfully exploiting these kind of arguments [of high profits] by U.S. firms', Leland L. Johnson, *U.S. Private Investment in Latin America: Some Questions of National Policy*, the RAND Corporation, Santa Barbara, Calif., July 1964, p. 54.

(4) *Interaffiliate debt–equity strategy*[17]

Intercountry income distribution in the presence of trans-national enterprises will be affected by, among other factors, the relationship that exists between interaffiliate debt and equity of their wholly owned subsidiaries. Payments for foreign debt usually imply a different tax treatment from that of remitted profits in the host countries with corresponding income effects for the latter. There are various reasons why transnational enterprises will prefer more interaffiliate debt rather than additional equity holding as a mechanism of company-originated sources of funds for the activities of their wholly owned affiliates.[18]

First, in the case of company nationalization, host countries have tended to 'honour' more the payment of the debt, rather than the equity, of expropriated foreign firms. This might be due to the host countries' association of debt repayment with their overall capacity for foreign indebtedness. Thus, in countries where foreign investors fear potential nationalization, they will tend to prefer debt rather than more equity holdings in existing subsidiaries. Second, the transformation of interaffiliate debt into equity is usually possible or even welcomed by host countries. The reverse, though, is not true because of fears of decapitalization. In this sense, companies have higher degrees of freedom by maintaining more interaffiliate debt rather than more equity investment in a wholly owned subsidiary. Third, where corporate taxes in the host countries are smaller than at home a firm might choose the payment of the principal of the debt as a mechanism of profit remission for which no additional taxes are paid at the home country. Such tax avoidance by firms introduces the repayment of the principal, in addition to the interest payments for debt, in income calculations. Thus, company preferences on interaffiliate debt–equity structures could have important effects on intercountry income distribution resulting from foreign direct investments loans from the same origin.

D. DIFFERENCES IN GOVERNMENT POLICIES AND THEIR EFFECTS ON TRANSFER PRICING

In the previous sections of the present chapter we assumed neutral government policies with respect to tariff rates on products

---

[17] I thank Professor Louis Wells, Jr., for his suggestions on the subject.

[18] Certain limits will exist due to the leverage effect of interaffiliate debt on the cost of external financing.

imported by foreign affiliates and profit tax rates. Furthermore, we assumed that foreign affiliates did not share equity with local investors and that no limits existed on profit remissions. We now relax these assumptions so as to evaluate the modifying effects they imply for our conclusions with respect to the relative-expenditures-requirements. We will not discuss the equivalent case involving the relative-investment-requirement since such analysis is quite straightforward: any cost for the company that arises from government policies has to be compared to the differentials of opportunity costs of capital confronting alternative investment opportunities in different countries. If the former costs are greater, then decisions based solely on the relative-investment-requirement will be reversed. If the latter costs are greater then such decisions will be maintained as originally stated. We proceed now to relax the assumptions that appeared on p. 99.

## (1) *External indirect fiscal charges (e.g. tariffs) and their effects on transfer pricing*

Intercountry income flows resulting from internal pricing practices of transnational enterprises can imply additional indirect fiscal payments for a company. For example, charging higher transfer prices on intermediate products or capital goods sold by a parent firm to its foreign subsidiary can imply reduction in the over-all returns of the enterprise because of higher tariff payments paid to the host country. Or higher royalties for technical assistance paid by a subsidiary to its parent can result in higher negotiation costs or remissions taxes paid to the host country. Such indirect fiscal effects constitute an important factor that, in some cases, could reverse the outcome of intracompany pricing that would have resulted from the fulfilment of the relative-expenditures-requirement analysed in section A.

Let $Y, t$, and $x$ stand as defined on p. 100 and 101. Also let $\tau$ stand for the average *ad valorem* tariff rate in a host country confronting the goods imported by a given firm from its foreign affiliates. Then, the enterprise will be indifferent as to where it declares its foreign earned income if $\tau = [(t(1 - x))/(1 - t)]$. The enterprise will pursue maximum transfer prices possible if $\tau < [(t(1 - x))/(1 - t)]$, and minimum ones if the opposite holds true.[19]

[19] For calculations see Appendix 4.

Hence if the relative-expenditures-requirement applies to the operations of a firm, transfer pricing in the presence of tariffs does not depend only on profit tax *differentials* among countries, as indicated in the footnote on p. 97, but also on the *absolute* level of tax rates. Only if $x = 100$ per cent, that is, only if all foreign earned income is declared as profit by the parent, will positive tariff rates result in the minimization of transfer prices in the absence of tax differentials. If profit tax rates converge to the 50 per cent mark, then the *ad valorem* tariff rates, which will leave the enterprise indifferent as to where it declares its profits, will be equal to the percentage of additional, foreign earned income which is *not* declared as profit by the firm.[20]

In conclusion, tariffs and other indirect fiscal charges can significantly influence the intracompany pricing policies of vertically integrated transnational enterprises. In situations of high tariffs on intermediate products imported by foreign subsidiaries and/or high percentages of profit declaration from foreign earned income and/or uniformly low corporate taxes, the indirect fiscal effects could reverse the policies that would have occurred under the strict application of the relative-expenditures-requirement. It is not surprising, then, that transnational enterprises often consider tariffs on goods imported by their subsidiaries as one of the most important negotiable elements upon which they condition their direct investments. It has been a frequent experience in Latin America that bargaining emphasis on such tariffs is more important than, for example, limits on profit remissions.

## (2) *Tax differentials among countries and interaffiliate charges*

Let $t_1$ indicate the tax rate in the home country of a transnational corporation and $t_2$ the equivalent rate in the host country of a wholly owned subsidiary. If $t_2 > t_1$ then, in addition to the relative-expenditures-requirement, tax differential considerations will prompt income remission through transfer pricing rather than profit repatriation taxed at higher rates. If $t_1 > t_2$ and credits for taxes paid abroad apply it is usually assumed that the enterprise will be indifferent between higher transfer pricing and profit remissions as long as tariffs are zero. Yet if the relative-expenditures-requirement applies to the parent's outlays (that is

[20] For example if $x = 70\%$ and $t = 50\%$ then $\tau = [(t(1 - x))/(1 - t)]$ when $\tau = 30\% = (1 - x)$.

if $x < 100$ per cent), then maximization of the global after-tax funds available to the firm will require the transfer of income from the subsidiary to the parent through interaffiliate charges as long as $t_1 < t_2 + (1 - x)$ and $t_2 > 0$. *It should be emphasized that such income transfers from the subsidiary to the parent will occur even if the profit tax rate confronting the latter is greater than that confronting the former, if the above conditions are met.*

To indicate the secondary importance of tax *differentials* among nations as compared to the overwhelming importance of the relative-expenditures-requirement on intercountry income distribution the following numerical example is presented. Assume $t_1 = 50\%$, $t_2 = 45\%$, and a transnational enterprise that declares 70% of the income repatriated from its subsidiaries as profit in the home country while the remaining 30% is used to cover expenses undertaken by the parent. Then, on the basis of an optimum after-tax profit strategy the firm will be induced to transfer untaxed income from the host country to that of the parent firm since $t_1 = 50\% < 45\% + (1 - 70\%) = 75\%$. The government of the host country, in order to stimulate income (and/or profit) declaration by foreign subsidiaries within its tax jurisdiction, decides to reduce drastically its corporate tax rate from 45 per cent to 25 per cent. Such a reduction, though, will still leave the transnational enterprise, given the above-cited conditions, in a state where it will be induced to transfer untaxed income (and/or profits) outside the subsidiary's country. Despite the low tax rate, the global financing needs of the firm will still require, in our example, the transfer of income to the parent's home country since $t_1 = 50\% < 25\% + (1 - 70\%) = 55\%$.

If non-zero tariffs and other indirect fiscal charges are introduced in a situation of tax differentials among countries where $t_1 > t_2$, then the enterprise will be indifferent as to where it declares its income if

$$\tau = \frac{t_2[1 - (t_1 - t_2) - x]}{1 - t_1 + t_2(t_1 - t_2)}$$

## (3) The effects of local participants

Let $p$ stand for the percentage participation of a transnational enterprise in the ownership of a joint venture. Then, if additional income earned by the joint venture is declared first as profit in the host country and then part of it is remitted to the foreign equity owners, the net after-tax funds available to the transnational enterprise will be $Y(1 - t)p$.

If, instead, income is transferred abroad through interaffiliate charges the equivalent funds available to the corporation will be $Y(1 - tx)$. Since $x \leqslant 100$ per cent, Case B will always be preferred to Case A in the absence of tariff payments. If indirect fiscal charges, though, are introduced, then the tariff rate for which the transnational corporation will be indifferent as to where it declares its income is:

$$\tau = \frac{t(p - x) + (1 - p)}{p(1 - t)}$$

It can be shown algebraically that this tariff rate is greater than the one applying to the case of wholly owned subsidiaries, which as estimated on p. 113 is $(t(1 - x))/(1 - t)$.

Thus, in joint ventures and in the absence of indirect fiscal charges, a foreign transnational enterprise will *always* prefer remission of income through transfer pricing to profit declaration in the host country. In the presence of tariffs, the latter need to be higher in the case of joint ventures than in foreign wholly owned subsidiaries, in order to reverse the decision of a transnational firm as to where it prefers to declare its income. The reason, obviously, rests on the fact that, in addition to tax payments, profit declaration by a joint venture implies the sharing of such profits with local participants. The higher propensity of a firm to transfer untaxed profit out of a joint venture through interaffiliate charges could be checked, though, by the potential control on decision-making exercised by the local participants. If, however, local participants are not able to influence the decisions on transfer pricing, *governments pursuing explicit or implicit policies which encourage joint ventures might paradoxically bring about, in the absence of other complementary policies, a higher transfer abroad of income generated in their countries by joint ventures than in the case of wholly owned subsidiaries.*

## (4) *Limits on profit repatriation*

Such limits are usually expressed as a percentage of invested capital rather than as a percentage of accrued profits. The restrictions imposed on remissions amount to an equivalent of 100 per cent taxation for profits above the repatriation ceiling if un-remitted profits from affiliates are considered of no use to the transnational enterprise. Such a strategy pursued by host countries could generate most serious policy-induced distortions in corporate behaviour. Firms will attempt to remit profits through any other channel that has an equivalent net result of less than 100 per cent leakage from corporate funds. Thus countries instituting limits on remission of profits by foreign corporations have to introduce other complementary policies to achieve their balance of payments or income objectives. *Otherwise it might happen that countries with limits on profit repatriation will end up with higher income and balance of payments outflows than without such remission limits.*

### E. QUALIFICATIONS AND CONCLUDING REMARKS

In the previous pages we presented a tax avoidance[21] model according to which transnational enterprises do not simply maximize yearly after-tax global profits but rather after-tax funds available to the firm. Such funds include not only declared returns but also income used to cover planned outlays. The latter, although constituting investments for global operations, appear as costs due to fiscal considerations. These reported costs assure the firm's long-run competitive survival and other objectives as much as business savings leading to reported investments. Furthermore, it is quite probable that during certain years firms 'create' expenditures. In the complexity of their objectives firms might not pursue a policy of reported profit maximization. Rather they might seek stable or steadily increasing profitability, given industry standards. Reported profit maximization could imply fluctuations of returns which during good years could attract the attention of labour unions, anti-trust authorities, or competitors. During lean years, after good ones, creditors (like banks) could consider such firms credit-risky because of the variance in their performance. Thus certain expenditures could serve as a buffer for unwarranted income fluctuations as much as they serve as investment outlays for future returns.

The availability of funds to finance certain key expenditures that, managed by transnational enterprises, appear to be highly

---

[21] Tax avoidance is obviously distinct from tax evasion. The latter implies actions contrary to established fiscal requirements and legislation while the former implies tax minimization within the established legal and administrative frameworks.

country-concentrated implies important direct intercountry income distribution effects. More so, though, their composition implies a particular bias in the international division of skilled labour and of knowledge with, in turn, important dynamic intercountry sharing of future global returns and intercountry dependence for growth.

Furthermore, other elements in the corporate strategy (such as technological ascendancy and barriers of entry through the effects of transfer pricing, interaffiliate debt–equity structures, etc.) imply additional considerations on intercountry income distribution. Such considerations are not easily incorporated in simple maximization functions but are more adequately understood within simulation models. All of the previous conclusions need to be qualified by the possible effect of diseconomies of scale on company behaviour resulting from rigidities in administrative rules, conflicting interests between departments or affiliates of the same parent, etc.

Finally, placing the above within an oligopoly model with a high interdependence of actions among participants further accentuates the complexity of corporate behaviour. Such behaviour is not only conditioned by home and host government policies, but it affects such policies given the weight that such firms have in the world economy. A better understanding of the effects of transnational enterprises will require not only an improvement in tools of economic analysis. It will also require a higher disclosure of elements of company operations such as their international cost allocations, their effects on government policies, their usage of diverse bargaining powers to affect country and factor distribution of returns, etc. Such disclosure will almost certainly affect the economic tools of analysis used.

# CHAPTER VII

# Bargaining and Foreign Factor Flows

A. SOME GENERAL COMMENTS ON BARGAINING

The foreign investor offers capital, know-how (technological and managerial), some opportunities of commercialization, and, among other possibilities, that of a certain structure of industrial development. The host country offers access to the home market (particularly in the manufacturing sector), access to natural resources (as in the extractive industries), and access to special comparative advantages (such as cheap labour). Such inputs to an investment project by both parties can lead to an agreement that is mutually beneficial. Other alternative production and ownership structures (like coproduction agreements, licensing arrangements, minority equity participation, profit sharing) can result in different configurations of benefits that could fall within the satisficing range of returns acceptable to both participants.[1]

The exercise of bargaining power depends, then, on the awareness of the size of the distributable returns (e.g. the size, among other things, of the effective taxable earnings rather than solely of the declared ones). It also depends on an evaluation of the different comparative strengths and possibilities for applying negotiating power over different periods of time, when there exist different degrees of dependence between foreign investors and host countries. Furthermore, the form or appearance in which bargaining power is exercised can in some cases be quite important. For example, a host country can decide not to permit payment of royalties for technology by subsidiaries to their foreign parents. This could be considered, by some, as quite restrictive to foreign investors. Unless there also exist limits on profit remissions, the same result can be achieved by taxing royalties at the same rate as profits to be remitted. The latter policy, having the same net

[1] See P. Streeten, 'The Multinational Enterprise and Development', mim., July 1972.

result, could be subject to different negotiable pressures by foreign firms.

Advice by economists often limits itself to different forms of benefit–cost estimates which in turn constitute forms of project or investment analysis. In the more sophisticated cases their conceptual origins can be traced in the literature of 'optimal' interest[2] and foreign exchange rates.[3] The approaches differ in areas such as the utilization of domestic cost estimates,[4] or of 'world price' equivalents, to measure costs and outputs.[5] Yet, quite generally, they follow a similar approach in applying cost–benefit analysis to each one of the participants *separately*.

On the basis of such analysis, if the net benefits for the host country exceed some minimum warranted returns, the conclusion is often reached (or implied) that foreign direct investment should be accepted rather than that it should be acceptable. The former implies that the 'alternative situation' is the absence of foreign direct investment, disregarding a multiplicity of negotiable situations where foreign direct investment could still be present. Furthermore it disregards the possibility of achieving other production and/or ownership combinations whose net benefits could be more acceptable for the host country *and* possible to achieve. Thus the unilateral application of benefit–cost analysis, which divorces itself from the actual and/or acceptable benefits accruing to the foreign factors supplier, reduces policy considerations in a passive state even if decisions among the participants are interdependent and opportunities potentially diverse. In another area where bargaining applies, that of trade unions, the equivalent application of benefit–cost analysis (as it is presently used in extreme cases in the foreign investment model) would have implied that any wage rate above subsistence level should be accepted.

[2] For a summary of approaches see P. D. Henderson, 'Investment Criteria for Public Enterprises', in R. Turvey (ed.), *Public Enterprise*, Penguin, Harmondsworth, 1968.

[3] For the corresponding literature survey see E. Bacha and L. Taylor, 'Foreign Exchange Shadow Prices: A critical Review of Current Theories', *Quarterly Journal of Economics*, vol. 85, no. 2 (May 1971).

[4] See M. Bruno, 'The Optimal Selection of Export-Promoting and Import-Substituting Projects', in United Nations, *Planning the External Sector: Techniques, Problems, and Policies*, ST/TAO/SECT/91, New York, 1967.

[5] See, for example, I. M. D. Little and J. A. Mirrless, *Manual of Industrial Project Analysis in Developing Countries*, Vol. II: *Social Cost Benefit Analysis*, OECD, Paris, 1969.

If, on the other hand, a bargaining framework is introduced (where partial benefit–cost analysis is one of the various tools used rather than the only objective of evaluation) then a series of alternative approaches and needs for comparison are available. Furthermore, the horizon of policy alternatives is significantly enhanced. For example, if a foreign investor enters in a country in order to protect an existing export market as a defensive strategy against other potential competitors who might plan the same or alternative production schemes in the host country (a frequent case implied in the product cycle theory), then the following occurs. From the point of view of the host country the total additional income effects from that particular investor do not constitute the relevant incremental benefits obtained. The latter amount to the difference, if any (positive or negative), between such an investment and alternative opportunities. Thus the opportunity cost for not receiving a particular investment is smaller than the total net income generated and equally smaller than the opportunity cost, under equivalent circumstances, of an expansive, new investment. Also from the point of view of the defensive investor, decisions are undertaken not on the basis of the difference between the incremental cost of supplying a market from, let us say, the home country and the average cost of producing abroad. Rather, decisions are based on the difference between total additional revenues and total additional costs in doing business abroad. Thus, in the case of a defensive investment a host country has less to gain from an additional investor than in the case of an expansive one, under comparable production situations. Also, given certain conditions of transportation costs and tariffs rates, the defensive investor has more to lose if he does not undertake the investment than in the case of an expansive activity. The difference in relative magnitudes could be quite significant to imply possibilities of additional gains for the host country through intelligent use of bargaining. Even small countries can find, in relative terms, their bargaining power significantly increased in confronting large transnational enterprises in situations like the one described above. A benefit–cost analysis applied unilaterally to the host country and omitting other production opportunities obscures such important policy alternatives.

In the manufacturing sector the negotiable elements involved with respect to foreign direct investments are multiple and of diverse kinds. We will be treating briefly below two critical ones, of particular relevance to developing countries. Others include exports of goods produced by foreign subsidiaries, the degree of obligatory content of local inputs, choice of appropriate processes given differences of social and private benefits, tax treatments (including depreciations and reserve allowances), pay/out ratios, royalty and other remissions, requirements for local participants in ownership and control, internal market control and price fixing, local labour training, extent of capitalization of intangibles, revaluations of assets due to currency devaluations, tariff rates on inputs imported, subsidies such as on energy, accounting inventory valuations due to inflation, other income reporting techniques, etc. All of these can be and often are translated into net cash flow effects by the foreign investors depending on managerial sophistication. Host countries, though, often apply piecemeal policies to each one of them (since they are handled by different legislative and administrative statures or agencies) although they represent a negotiable package.

The dynamics of bargaining, given the tools available, represent almost a *continuous process of distributional performance* between the host nation and the foreign investor. For example, progressive application of obligatory content of local inputs implies continuous distributional effects among participants. Furthermore, host government policies with effects on such income distribution can be direct and all-encompassing, as through the effective protection offered to production activities where foreign subsidiaries participate. Or they can be direct and specific, such as through the requirements on domestic participation in the ownership of firms,[6] through direct price controls on imported intermediate products for further processing by foreign owned corporations, etc.[7]

We come now to discuss two areas where bargaining, in the context of foreign direct investment, has a significant impact on direct intercountry income distribution.

The first refers to the relationship, raised frequently in previous chapters, between tariff policies, particularly those of developing

---

[6] See articles 27–37 of Decision no. 24 of the Andean Pact.

[7] See policies of the Instituto de Comercio Exterior of Colombia or the equivalent policies of the U.S. Internal Revenue Service Code, No. 492.

countries, and the presence of foreign direct investors. The manner by which import substitution was implemented by host countries found in various cases a strong supporter and inducer in the case of transnational firms. Infant industry arguments were, thus, used not only for domestic factors of production but they were effectively extended to apply such infancy to enterprises like General Motors, ICI, Mitshubishi, Philips International, etc., which dominate national industries. Also inappropriate policies on high tariff and non-tariff protection were often based on the difficulty of sorting out, through relevant cost accounting analysis, two different elements: (a) the diseconomies of small-scale production; and (b) the channels of effective remission (such as transfer pricing or payments for know-how, trademarks, etc.) which appear as costs in the income statements of the protected wholly owned foreign affiliates. The latter costs constitute negotiable elements where quite often no market price equivalents exist. (Studies undertaken by O.E.C.D. in various automotive industries in developing countries found in some cases that the import content, supplied by affiliated firms, was greater than the 'international' price of the finished goods. Protection in this industry has generally been explained on the basis of scale considerations.)

The second area of bargaining to be mentioned is that between foreign direct investments and technology importation. The former constitutes one of the principal mechanisms by which industrially applied technology is presently being transmitted. It includes not only process know-how but also training and transmission of over-all technical knowledge to the subsidiary as well as to its local suppliers of inputs or users of outputs.

Foreign direct investments, given alternative opportunities in the technology market, can contribute significantly to the industrial application of know-how in their host countries. Yet to the extent that foreign direct investments might involve a process of transmission of knowledge similar to that of turn-key arrangements, they could also have some important technology-retarding effects for the host country. The rational preference of foreign investors to transmit a package of technological inputs (e.g. feasibility and other consulting type of studies, engineering design, plant design and lay-out, product design, packaging specifications, tool and machinery requirements, etc.) could in itself prove to be counter to the long-run interests of the receiving country.[8] Such 'peripheral' technology (as contrasted to the 'core' technology involved in process know-how) implies fixed costs in learning and development and constitute important prerequisites of industrial development through skill differentiation. Thus, although a country might benefit in a particular project by importing such non-captive, industry-non-specific know-how embodied in foreign direct investments, it could incur significant costs over time, given similar requirements for future projects.

Research recently undertaken in Japan[9] indicated that since the early 1950s, given that country's technological infrastructure, the government (in exchange for access to the domestic market) negotiated the importation of know-how in a manner that achieved a fairly thorough disaggregation of technical inputs. (Such disaggregation was often negotiated and provided by the foreign factor-suppliers.) Domestic supply of some of them was negotiated with the foreign enterprises even if this implied initially subsidized technological efforts in that country. Over a period of time, though, such a policy contributed to the creation of an engineering capacity that could serve various sectors even if the country continued to be dependent on foreign inflows in process know-how.[10]

To understand the dynamics of bargaining, within the foreign investment model and in particular the bargaining process for technology (tied or not to foreign capital) it is necessary to understand that supply estimates (that is the cost structure facing the host country) *cannot be determined a priori*. We can refer to the supply (as distinct from availability) of capital and/or technology only with respect to the one facing a given firm with a particular size and ownership structures; confronting a given effective market protection related to goods produced as well as imported

---

[8] Ignacy Sachs has called the direct importation of elements of technology without filtering them through the receiving country's technological infrastructure 'pseudo-transfers' of know-how.

[9] The research was carried out by Juan Tampier under contract with the Junta del Acuerdo de Cartagena.

[10] In the early and middle 1960s Japan continued to be almost totally dependent on U.S. process technology in the petrochemicals industry. Yet, from acquired knowledge in the engineering requirements of oil refineries they negotiated the utilization of domestic inputs for engineering in petrochemicals, often with some foreign specifications. This knowledge in turn contributed in the late 1960s to the development of Japan's own petrochemicals know-how.

for further processing; operating within a particular fiscal and monetary system; and confronting specific government policies with respect to access and negotiations for capital and technology acquisition. Thus, for example, for the same know-how a Chilean-owned firm confronts a different supply of technology from a Brazilian-owned firm or a foreign-owned firm in Chile or Brazil. The issue becomes even more complex if one considers the fact that the supply of more of the same technology is meaningless for a given firm once it has mastered that technology and is contractually and legally permitted to use it.

The following example will help to clarify the reasons for the *a priori* interdeterminancy, in the case of technology, of its cost (or supply). The predominant form in which the price of technology is determined is by a percentage rate on the sale of goods or services incorporating the respective know-how. To start with, such a percentage for a given technology will depend on—among other factors—whether the recipient firm is owned by the licensor or by third parties. If it is owned by the licensor and the local government does not intervene in the process of negotiations, the percentage of royalty payments will depend on the global financial management of the parent-licensor. As discussed in previous chapters, if the corporate tax rate in the host country of the subsidiary is higher than that of the home country, the parent will be induced to increase royalty receipts so as to reduce over-all tax payments for the firm. Similarly, the higher the *ad valorem* tariff rates for intermediate products sold by the parent to a subsidiary, the lower will the (transfer) pricing of such products tend to be; this in turn will tend to prompt higher royalty payments as a mechanism of income transfer. The considerations confronting the supply of the same technology for a firm not owned by the licensor will be quite different. Furthermore, the cost of technology (whether referring to percentage rates or absolute amounts) will depend on the number of units sold and the price of the product incorporating the respective know-how. Also, given a royalty rate, the higher the *ad valorem* tariff rate on the products produced by a given know-how, the higher will the absolute cost for obtaining that technology tend to be.

This *a priori* indeterminancy of the supply of technology often reduces accepted concepts or definitions on the subject to totally arbitrary meanings. One of these concepts is the so-called 'technological balance of payments' of countries. It is defined as the net effect on the balance of payments of a country resulting from the receipts and payments from the sale and purchase of technology with the rest of the world. For countries like Japan, the term technological balance of payments makes some sense, even if it is not adequately representative since it omits the payments for technology through intermediates and capital goods embodying (or not) technology. This is so since technology is imported basically by Japanese-owned firms. In the case, though, of developing countries where the largest part of contractually imported technology is handled via foreign-owned affiliated firms the term 'technological balance of payments' could represent totally arbitrary notions.

For a transnational enterprise intra-firm transfers of income through royalty payments; profit remissions, prices of goods exchanged between affiliates, interest payments for interaffiliate debt, etc. respond to a process of adjustment to government economic policies and to external competitive as well as political pressures. As indicated earlier, only the total package of returns to the foreign factor suppliers could give a more adequate figure. Even in that case, though, the apparent arbitrariness of the costs for the host country will not be eliminated completely since, for *each* particular recipient country, one does not take into account the global strategy of the transnational enterprise. In that context it is only for the firm that arbitrariness need not exist in the setting of prices for the usage of resources. The issues raised above can be seen in the following hypothetical example. The latter need not be all that atypical since it depicts one of the main advantages of transnational firms, namely their ability to mobilize resources from around the globe and use them in areas where such firms have the highest needs.

During a given year the subsidiary of a foreign company in Brazil might pay royalties to its Mexican affiliate since the latter had, during that year, especially high expenditure requirements and, thus, the parent temporarily sublicensed to Mexico various patent rights. The next year the Brazilian subsidiary might need company funds for a certain expansion and as a result royalties might be totally eliminated to take advantage of the lower corporate tax rate granted in that country as compared with that of the parent. The third, fourth, etc., years' royalties could be paid to the parent or an affiliate in France for technology acquired by the Brazilian subsidiary several years before. That technology could have been developed or not by the parent and the process of its adaptation to Brazil could have involved additional costs or not. Furthermore, the size of royalty payments could have been basically determined by the needs of the parent or of the French affiliate to set up, for example, new marketing projects in products completely unrelated to those of the Brazilian firm. The net result, for Brazil, is an element of the country's 'technological balance of payments'!

Recent experience in the extractive industries (particularly in the petroleum sector) has indicated very significant advances in intercountry income distribution in favour of the producing, developing countries. Given market and risk considerations, such advances were achieved to a large extent by overcoming the (economists') preoccupation with benefit–cost analysis applied to *each one* of the participating parties and by directing evaluation to the package of the accrued returns to both sides. In addition, a significant shift in bargaining power has been achieved through explicit search and use of information (understanding, that is, the industry's economics) and by the application of collective power. In the manufacturing sector, on the other hand, given sectorial differences, the understanding of the bargaining context in negotiating with foreign investors has advanced, comparatively, very little.

One of the basic factors that has blurred the proper understanding and exercise of bargaining by developing countries in this area is their critical weakness of lacking diverse forms of industrial technology. In many instances the scarcity of domestic capital or foreign exchange reserves as needed for an investment can hardly be compared to the domestic scarcity of technical know-how required. In many respects one can draw parallel examples between the experience of developing countries in the extractive sector during the first decades of the century and their approach to technology acquisition during the 1960s and 1970s. In the remaining sections of this chapter we will present first a brief description of the experience of a country such as Colombia in explicitly introducing the exercise of bargaining in the purchase of technology. We will then conclude by singling out some of the parallel experiences of developing countries in managing concessions in the extractive industries in the first part of the twentieth century and in handling the licensing of technology in the past two decades.

## B. A BRIEF DESCRIPTION OF THE EXPERIENCE OF THE COLOMBIAN COMITÉ DE REGALÍAS

In 1967, as part of the over-all exchange control mechanisms introduced in Colombia, a Comité de Regalías was established to negotiate and approve all contracts of technology purchase for that country. The members of this committee, other than its permanent secretariat, included permanent representatives from each of the principal agencies which administered the different aspects of the over-all exchange control policy. They included: (1) a representative of the National Planning Department whose function in the latter institution was to approve all foreign investments in Colombia; (2) the chief legal officer of the Balance of Payments Division of the Banco de la Republica who controlled, together with the chief economic officer, all balance of payments transactions of the country concerning the private sector; (3) a representative of the agency (INCOMEM) that authorizes the importation of goods and administers tariff and other protection for Colombia; (4) the head of the industrial property division (and related matters) of the Ministry of Development; and (5) a representative of the agency of the Prefectura de Cambios whose function included the control of discriminatory pricing of goods and services imported or exported from Colombia. This negotiating body was assisted by a group of engineers, lawyers, and economist-accountants who prepared preliminary opinions on company presented material. Such material was evaluated on the basis of some explicit methodological requirements prepared by the committee with respect to the technical, legal, and economic conditions and effects of each know-how contract.

The Comité de Regalías based its negotiations on the government's power to permit or reject access to the domestic market. It thus combined policies on treatment of technology (within or outside the foreign investment model) with the conditions of entry in the local market. This type of power seldom resides within the limits of private firms. (Exceptions exist as in the case of patent privileges.) It is of interest to note that no case occurred in which a foreign technology and/or capital supplier withdrew on his own account from the Colombia market because of the negotiations undertaken by the Colombian government.

From the second half of 1967 to June 1971 the Comité de Regalías of Colombia evaluated 395 contracts of technology commercialization. Of these, 334 were negotiated, modified, and finally approved and 61 were rejected. In the process of negotiations, payment of royalties were reduced by about 40 per cent or about U.S. $8,000,000 for 1970. This annual royalty reduction in Colombia through government negotiation was equivalent to the total explicit annual payments for technology reported for the whole economy of Chile.

In Colombia it was estimated that the average absolute size of royalties negotiated with foreign subsidiaries was three times as large as those paid by national firms. This can be attributed to differences in the volume of sales of given products, differences in the number of products included in contracts, and differences in percentage royalty rates agreed upon. In the negotiations that took place between the middle of 1967 and the end of 1969 of the contracts that were approved as presented (rather than being modified or rejected) 75 per cent had as licensees nationally owned firms. Unless the Comité de Regalías applied easier standards to nationally owned firms, this tends to suggest that such firms underwent a much more rigorous negotiating process with their foreign licensors before presenting contracts for approval to the Comité de Regalías. Or it could equally suggest that foreign-owned subsidiaries in Colombia were using royalty payments as an alternative to profit repatriation and not for the compensation of strictly defined technical services, with significant fiscal and balance of payments effects for Colombia.

In addition, during the latter part of 1970 and the beginning of 1971 negotiations by the Colombian Comité de Regalías:

1. reduced by 90 per cent the tie-in clauses in the purchase of intermediates;
2. eliminated by 100 per cent the restrictive export clauses;
3. reduced by 80 per cent clauses on minimum royalty payments;
4. prohibited payments on taxes by the licensee on royalties remitted to the licensor;
5. established maximum percentage royalty rates by sectors.

These significant achievements by the Comité de Regalías must be qualified as follows: as far as foreign-owned subsidiaries are concerned reduction in royalty payments could result either in higher profits which could be remitted after payment of local taxes or they could be passed on to the parent firm through interaffiliate transfer pricing. Furthermore, the exclusion of clauses from the contract of a subsidiary does not mean that the practices involved will be abolished, since control through ownership could still dictate the same practices. As far as nationally owned firms are concerned, it is known that in some cases after such government intervention, "gentlemen's agreements" exist, extra-contractually, between licensors and licensees. Nevertheless, in other cases, government intervention has resulted in known benefits for nationally owned firms.

The Colombian Comité de Regalías confronted three basic problems, one inherent in any negotiating body and two particular to the tasks of this specific committee. The first refers to the potential corruption of government officials. Regulatory agencies, whether in developed or developing countries, have often been known to collude with the parties they are supposed to regulate. Specific examples of attempts to bribe members of the Comité de Regalías were encountered during our research in Colombia. The major institutional resistance to such practices was due to the multi-individual and multi-agency checks applied on this committee. Distinct evaluations were prepared by the committee's specialists and separate opinions were given by each one of the members of the negotiating body. Since each of these members belonged to a government agency which also evaluated, although within different scopes, diverse elements related to the importation of technology and foreign capital, the individual's opinions and the committee's decisions were subject to further evaluation (at a higher level) by other government bodies. Thus, a foreign technology supplier would have had to bribe the staffs of six different government agencies in order to secure collusion. Still, however, since the Comité de Regalías enjoys considerable power, the potential of some form of corruption exists. The ageing of the committee as time passes may show its susceptibility to such policy-induced distortions.[11]

[11] Discussions in the Colombian government indicated that the age of members of the Comité de Regalías (most of them fairly young technicians) was a positive factor

A second basic problem of the Comité de Regalías was that of confronting each foreign supplier of a particular technology more or less as a monopolist. No attempt was made on the part of the committee explicitly to search for alternative sources in the international market or to collect data from international information centres. Only when more than one supplier was presented concurrently, or when previous negotiations offered comparisons, was there an opportunity for judging among alternative situations. The question of planned international search for knowledge and its alternative sources of supply could institutionally prove to be of the highest importance. Very few transnational firms have developed, themselves, the greater part of the technological knowledge they employ. Rather, they search continuously and methodologically the international market and pay close attention to the development of their competitors. Such an activity is complementary to, rather than a substitute for, internal R & D efforts. The best innovators are usually capable of being also the best imitators.[12]

The third shortcoming of the committee, during its first three years of negotiations, was its predominant orientation towards balance of payments issues and, as its name indicates, that only with respect to royalties. Yet subsequent negotiations tied royalty payments to an understanding of imported product pricing. Also, with the request for and approval of complementary supportive legislation conscious efforts were made to control restrictive business practices that originated from contracts of technology commercialization.

## C. CONCESSION AGREEMENTS IN THE EXTRACTIVE INDUSTRIES AND LICENSING CONTRACTS ON TECHNOLOGY COMMERCIALIZATION

Descriptive models on concession agreements in the extractive industries usually include, among others, the following general areas of consideration applying to the initial periods of agreement in the first half of this century.[13]

in the honesty of its operations. Of course, no conclusive evidence exists that corruption or protection of the 'national interest' is a function of a person's age.

[12] For an effort in this direction by developing countries see the policies and institutional organization included in Decision 24 of the Andean Pact.

[13] See for example L. T. Wells, Jr., in 'The Evolution of Concession Agreements',

1. The host country negotiating from weakness. 'Excessive permissiveness' in initial agreements.

2. Lack of knowledge of other agreements.

3. Competence of negotiating government officials and lack of institutional infrastructures.

4. Defensive negotiations and the element of time in progressive bargaining over different periods.

We proceed to discuss the parallel experiences of developing countries in the negotiations of concession agreements in the extractive sector and the licensing contracts on technology.

(1) *The host country negotiating from weakness. 'Excessive permissiveness' in initial agreements*

As in the case of concession agreements developing countries approach the initial negotiations for technology purchase from a position of considerable weakness. The main way in which a plant could be technologically viable might depend on its being designed on the basis of processes supplied from the outside; the only legal way by which a product might be manufactured could be through the licensing of the patent that covers that product or its process; the key factor in the competitive viability of a firm could be the necessary foreign technical assistance. Developing countries lacking basic technological infrastructure *have* to purchase know-how from the technologically endowed world. In this manner the late-latecomers can potentially increase their real rate of growth through the use of advancements in science and technology which were translated into product and process innovations in other countries. Until they have mastered the already available technology or until they are able to copy foreign techniques or develop their own they are dependent and hence in a very weak initial negotiating position. Such a weakness is reflected in the empirical results presented in earlier chapters that relate to negotiable (but not negotiated) elements such as export restrictions, tie-in clauses and the resulting price effects, other forms of restrictive business practices, etc. The appearance of these conditions constitutes the general case rather than the exception for countries like the members of the Andean Pact.

An understanding of these negotiable terms requires a distinc-

---

paper presented at the Harvard Development Advisory Service Conference, Sorrento, Italy, 1968, and R. Vernon, 'Long Run Trends in Concession Contracts', *American Journal of International Law* 61 (1967).

tion between various types of bargaining. For example, the bargaining power to attract foreign investors is probably, to a large extent, a function of a country's size and growth rate of the market, as well as of its access to third markets (e.g. U.S. investments in Belgium served as an entry to the EEC; recently a North American firm invested in Chile as a means of establishing, through Chile, a foothold in and use of its trade-mark in the socialist countries of Eastern Europe). However, bargaining power to control the practices of foreign investors and obtain more appropriate distribution of the generated net benefits probably depends on the degree of sophistication of the government machinery as well as on the government's political and economic design to intervene in the operations of foreign firms. Undoubtedly there are areas of overlapping effects between these two types of bargaining power. Yet a large part is quite distinct and necessitates different types of evaluating techniques as well as different forms of policies to achieve the results that are pursued. *Access* to market by foreign factor-suppliers and *treatment* of foreign investors and technology owners are two different issues with several distinct aspects.

The history of concession agreements teaches us that during the initial periods of these agreements, governments 'have been known to be incredibly permissive, at least when judged by hindsight ... In Latin America until World War I, concessionaires could usually count on nominal income tax rates, waivers of import duties and insignificant obligations ... Nominal as these commitments were, concessionaires were known to bargain hard in order to get them lower still.'[14]

Permissiveness on the part of the government of the host country in the purchase of technology is exemplified not only by its negotiating position (or lack of it) with respect to restrictive business practices (which usually refer to the conduct of business enterprises), but also by the way it confronts practices or behaviour that result from the structural characteristics of such enterprises[15] with reference to relative size and power, ownership ties, etc. For example, it is not uncommon to encounter cases where foreign wholly owned subsidiaries have capitalized in their books technology that originated from the parent corporation. As

[14] R. Vernon, op. cit., p. 83.
[15] See UNCTAD, 'Restrictive Business Practices', TD/B/C.2/54, Oct. 1968, p. 4.

a result they could be: (a) paying royalties; (b) reducing tax payments through depreciation charges of intangible assets; (c) having lower tax coefficients in countries where taxable profits are related to invested capital;[16] and (d) claiming higher capital repatriations; all for the same know-how. Clearly a foreign-owned subsidiary does not need to capitalize technology since 100 per cent of its capital is already owned by its parent. Thus, unless a government body intervenes between the 'private contracting' of a parent and a subsidiary, the distribution of returns from the use of technology is likely to be only one-sided.

Another case of permissiveness refers to the manner in which royalties are treated. Royalty rates are almost exclusively nominated and negotiated as a percentage of net sales. An $X$ per cent on the sale price of a certain commodity implies that royalties are being paid not only for the technology embodied in the intermediate products used and so on, but also for the protective tariff of the final product imposed by the government, the advertising expenses of the company, etc. Thus, the higher the final product tariffs, or the higher the advertising expenses of a company, or the higher its production inefficiency, the larger the absolute level of royalties paid for technology that originated abroad. Furthermore, the determination of royalties as a percentage of sales reduces the perceived size of these royalties. A 5 per cent or a 10 per cent royalty appears to be rather acceptable or logical. Yet, royalty payments as indicated in Chapter IV amounted to 600 per cent, 142 per cent, and 52 per cent of declared profits for parts of the Colombian pharmaceutical, chemical, and rubber industry respectively. Should not royalty rates be viewed by firms with respect to their profits and by governments with respect to domestic value added rather than with respect to sales?

As in the case of concession agreements, 'nominal as the commitments of the foreign investors are, [licensors] are known to bargain hard in order to get them lower still.'[16a] It is not uncommon in the experience of licensing agreements in Colombia and Chile to have the licensor—after for example, he has been guaranteed an implicit return of 15 per cent or 20 per cent on sales through intermediate product overpricing—bargain very hard to

[16] See G. J. Eder, J. C. Chommie, and H. J. Becerra, *Taxation in Colombia*, World Tax Series, Harvard Law School, Cambridge, Mass., 1964.

[16a] R. Vernon, op. cit., p. 83.

increase his royalty receipts from 5 per cent to 5·5 per cent on sales. Tax and accounting experts are specially flown to the developing country to bargain hard for the 0·5 per cent in royalty increase even if a many times multiple return has been secured through other arrangements.[17]

It appears that sellers of technology bargain very hard on small differences of royalty rates as a strategic choice that leaves other much more important negotiable aspects outside the negotiating process. The government or company negotiator concentrates his attention and negotiable trade-offs on elements that are perhaps completely marginal. By defining royalties as the only cost of technology purchase (since they are explicit) one overlooks the more important implicit costs such as intermediate product overpricing.

## (2) *Lack of knowledge of other agreements*

Acceptable competitive market conditions assume *a priori* sufficient and equitably available information. Yet in a bargaining framework information is an instrument upon which the whole system of relative power is based since the latter (i.e. bargaining power) is, among other things, a function of the knowledge of what the counterpart is gaining from different configurations of policies and situations. Furthermore, acquisition of information implies certain costs which need to be evaluated in relation to the benefits to be received. Thus, availability of information cannot be assumed as given but needs to be introduced as one of the policy variables in a country's confrontation with foreign investors. The economics of knowledge in the foreign investment model, an area quite unexplored, could show the possibilities and limits of exercising certain bargaining pressures.

The history of concession agreements teaches us that in the early stages of such agreements it was, quite often, practically impossible to obtain copies of the actual documents of the terms of the concession. Several countries considered concession agreements as secret documents and hence non-available to anyone except the negotiators. In other countries concession agreements were defined as, theoretically at least, in the public domain, but only a very small number of copies were reproduced and hence know-

[17] Several examples of this sort have been cited or experienced by the author during his association with the Colombian Committee of Royalties.

ledge of them was very restricted. If the countries themselves did not make available information to their public and to each other, clearly the foreign companies would not go against their self-interest and publish the terms of agreements. Quite the contrary: 'only a great deal of detective work—combing legal libraries of universities in developed countries, scanning trade journals for clues, trading information with other governments, etc.—could yield much information.'[18] It took some time to understand the necessity of exchanging information as an explicit policy by governments of developing countries. This, together with other factors, led to the establishment of such institutions as the Organization of Petroleum Exporting Countries (OPEC), which has as one of its main functions the dissemination of information to the definite interest of the member countries. The result of this enhanced availability of information led, together with market and risk factors, to the signing of 'model contracts' in the post-war period, like the ones by the government of Libya.

Reflecting on the process and procedures, with respect to information handling of technology commercialization during the 1960s, one encounters cases which are similar or parallel to the standards practised during the initial concession contracts. Due to mis-specified concepts of confidentiality and secrecy, contracts of technology purchase are kept completely secret. In countries that do not have application of an exchange control mechanism in contractual agreements, information is restricted to the two contracting parties. In countries where government regulating bodies intervene in the contractual processes between private parties, inadequately functioning administrative procedures limit the degree of knowledge of contractual terms. The members of royalty committees, usually, in an intuitive sense only, and by memory, know over-all industry terms. Of course, no explicit mechanism exists for intercountry comparisons. Governments very scrupulously guard the contractual agreements of their nationals from other neighbour countries, thinking that in that way they preserve national interests. Effectively, what they jointly achieve is a reduction of their own knowledge and bargaining power by segmenting the market of information and accentuating problems of relative ignorance. Government agencies in groups could certainly proceed to inform themselves about

[18] L. T. Wells, Jr., op. cit., p. 6.

market conditions in technology commercialization around the world as well as inform each other about it and about terms of agreements in their own countries. The benefits derived from such a policy could certainly outweigh the actual or imaginary gains from secrecy among nations on their contracts with foreign technology suppliers.

In addition to and in relation to the above, countries could introduce the use of the 'most favoured nation' principle. (This principle has been in use in international trade arrangements, like the GATT, and lately in the concessions' area.[19] The collectivity of a number of countries can reinforce the interests of the member nations if terms lower in one of them would also apply to others for contracts of 'similar' technology. An explicit introduction of such a clause could open the way to renegotiations. The whole system of most favoured nation could, actually, be an indirect way of achieving a common front for purchasing technology in an environment where negotiations by nature or by intent differ in points of time.

### (3) *Competence of negotiating government officials and lack of institutional infrastructure*

One of the factors that contributed to the relative weakness of government officials in their negotiations of initial concession agreements was the sheer inadequate understanding of the complex financial bookkeeping practices of the large multinational companies. In-depth analyses of concession agreements demonstrate cases where tax authorities were quite unprepared to deal with the issues of transfer pricing between parent and subsidiaries as a means of shifting untaxable profits from one country to another.

The terms of the early income tax agreements in some countries may appear very strange to those used to sophisticated tax systems. Government officials sometimes agreed to both depreciation and tax deductions of reserves for replacement of the same asset, tax liability to be determined by foreign accounting firms whose accounting principles were those of the shareholder and not those of a tax authority, allowance of

---

[19] See actions of the Federal Government of Nigeria in 1967 based on the 'most favoured African nation clause', OPEC, 'Collective Influence in the Recent Trends Towards Stabilization of International Crude and Product Prices'.

deduction for interest designed to permit tax-free shifting of profits outside of the host country, and so on and so on. Government negotiators found terms which they did not understand, or, for a fee (perhaps in the form of loans for shares or well paying positions on boards of directors) [accepted] terms which they were fairly certain their superiors or political opposition would not understand.[20]

The above passage could equally well be applied to technology commercialization, if one substituted licences of industrial know-how for concession agreements. Quite often the complexity of evaluating modern technology further aggravates any already existing inadequacies in financial analysis which translates technical coefficients to economic units of measurement. In the case of transfer pricing of intermediate (technology-embodying) products questions arise as to whether government officials are competent or not to handle this matter, as well as to whether an institutional framework exists which could attempt to scrutinize transfer prices. Also, as was indicated earlier, foreign wholly owned subsidiaries capitalize know-how for reasons not related to control. The companies pay royalties, have depreciation charges on intangible assets, and reduce their excess profit tax base through the capitalization of the same know-how.

In the process of evaluating and negotiating the purchase of foreign technology government officials are called upon to perform a dual task. First, they try or should try to scrutinize technology commercialization within a complex of other resources that are being jointly sold, like intermediate products or machinery. (If more sophistication is used to determine opportunity costs then they should evaluate, in addition, the complex of other resources or inputs whose use is being forgone or, in various cases, displaced.) Furthermore, a given technology is tied in with the transfer of capital, the extent of market opportunities (i.e. export restrictions), as well as the ability or inability to use other forms of complementary or substituting technology. Even more, technology commercialization is related to the tax system that regulates distribution of net benefits, the tariff policy that determines the extent of effective protection, etc. Evaluation of the

[20] L. T. Wells, Jr., 'The Evolution of Concession Agreements', pp. 9–10. Wells makes specific reference to such 'very strange' terms that exist in clauses of contracts between the Republic of Liberia and the Bethlehem Steel Corporation, the Liberian Mining Company, Ltd., and the Liberian American Swedish Minerals Company.

purchase of a given technology should thus try to scrutinize the whole package of interrelated effects of various inputs as well as policies and their implications, rather than limit itself to the explicit elements such as royalties, direct employment effects, direct balance of payments effects, etc. Social scientists, often in the pursuit of first-best recommendations, have been led to an excessive employment of *ceteris paribus* assumptions. This, in turn, has probably misdirected professionals to very marginal evaluation techniques. What is needed is not an analysis on *ceteris paribus* terms but a conceptualization of 'the problem as a whole to identify the ceteris'.[21]

Second, technology (or its process of commercialization) appears to be the least identified and understood factor of production. The form of its exchange takes place in the most vague manner to the minds, at least, of the purchasers. Countries have developed specific definitions as well as elaborate systems (which still leave much to be desired) for the classification and evaluation of the transfer of other resources. One need not spend very much time in a central bank or a customs office to notice the elaborate mechanisms of registration, classification, etc., of the transfer of financial capital or goods among countries. Generally, know-how is still commercialized under the broad, vague, and in many ways non-understood (economic-wise) word, 'technology'. Tautologically, we define the importation of technology as the importation of know-how. The question arises as to what, at least operationally, is the technology that a country is importing for a given industry, or process, or product.

An attempt to distinguish, for negotiating purposes, the different components that are brought together under the broad term of technology was initiated by the Colombian Comité de Regalías in 1970 and was formalized by Decision 24 of the Andean Pact. This included first, a separation of elements of industrial property (e.g. patents and trade-marks) and strictly technological components of a contract. With respect to the latter, an effort was made, where possible, to distinguish between production manuals supplied only once, at the beginning of a licensing agreement, continuous technical assistance over time, technology embodied in intermediates and capital goods imported, etc. Since technology lacks units of measurement, instead of negotiating payments for

[21] See Y. Aharoni, *The Foreign Investment Decision Process*, p. ix.

the above disaggregated components of know-how as a percentage of sales, Decision 24 established that negotiations should be undertaken with respect to the contribution of foreign technology to the profitability of recipient firms. For example, a cost-saving imported technology will be negotiated with respect to its effects on increasing net returns rather than as a percentage of total sales. Effects of profitability for the firm, and on value added for the host country, will determine the imputed value of technology. This, in turn, will determine the maximum permissible price to be paid for that technology. In addition to this imputed value, for the commercialization of know-how, one needs to determine the price equivalent of comparable technologies in different markets around the world. It is not uncommon that the same type of product can be produced by more than one process. Furthermore, and of great importance to developing countries, there are many different sources of supply, with different prices, that can offer a given type of technology for the kind of industrial needs that these countries have. (France, for example, might need computer technology that only IBM can provide, and Japan might need know-how that only Texas Instruments Co. has, but textiles technology, fertilizer plants, components for television sets, and processes for producing tyres have no great secrets and are available world-wide.) For developing countries, the opportunity cost of technology in the process of its commercialization (not its imputed value), can be determined only through the knowledge of available alternative sources of supply and their respective prices. Provisions for such action, through explicit search in the international market, were included in Decision 24 of the Andean Pact.

(4) *Defensive negotiations and the element of time in progressive bargaining over different periods*

In the history of concession agreements, the initial demands of the concessionary have been described as being based on the 'exaggerated emphasis of the defensive negotiator'.[22] Once an agreement is reached and capital is invested the bargaining power of the foreign concessionary clearly diminishes. He thus attempts to use his bargaining power right at the outset, when it is strongest. Furthermore, consistent with the tactics of the 'defensive negotia-

---

[22] R. Vernon, 'Long Run Trends in Concession Contracts', p. 84.

tor', initial terms are expected to be higher than the average ones during the life of the contract. The concessionary *expects* his initial terms to be reduced.

In principle, technology bought at a given period and sunk investments are quite similar notions if they are evaluated over a time range. Both of them are irreversible in time. The use of information during one period certainly does not diminish its availability in the future. On the contrary, its 'availability' is enhanced as it is being mastered, and once mastered, it cannot be lost. Thus, reacquisition of the same information in some future period involves, intrinsically, no additional cost, since this information is already embodied in machines, processes, and people's skills used in the past.

This property of decreasing imputed costs over time generates conflicting interests and varying degrees of dependence between supplier and recipient of information since its worth depends strictly on the point of time that is being evaluated. If history then repeats itself, the licensor probably is setting his initial terms 'on the exaggerated emphasis of the defensive negotiator' and expects his terms to be lowered, but not without hard bargaining. The renegotiations undertaken by the Colombian Comité de Regalías (whose results were presented in the previous pages) and the notes included in the minutes of this committee gave support to this conclusion.

A more explicit introduction of the time factor in the strategy of the government, or company negotiator of the developing country, has definite implications on his expected hehaviour. First, he has explicitly to define his negotiating horizon over a relevant time period where subsequent renegotiations will take into account the continuously shifting power and/or dependence relationship. What should be maximized is not the use of negotiating power at the initial negotiation, but the use of changing negotiating power over time. Second, the negotiator from the developing country should pre-plan the institutional means by which renegotiations can be opened so as to avoid alienating potential new technology suppliers by the negative effects of forced renegotiations. Clauses in the initial contract should exist which will smooth the road for the opening of negotiations. (In previous pages the 'most favoured contract' clause was indicated as an example.)

In addition, with respect to technology purchases, he should very carefully tie payments to received benefits from the know-how bought. As discussed earlier, quite often contracts on technology are signed without any differentiation of payments for patents, technical assistance, plant designs, etc. Clearly, as suggested in part 3 above, each one of these has a different incremental contribution to the buyer at different time periods. For example, in the pharmaceutical industry, technical assistance is quite often limited to a production manual which can be learned very quickly, while the key to the technology buyer's dependence on the seller is the patent covering the product or its process. By differentiating the types of know-how received, allocating payments for each one of them separately and indicating different time periods of duration for each one, the negotiator not only rationalizes his procedure of technology purchase, but also smooths the way to renegotiations at different time intervals.

# Concluding Remarks

AN analysis of the economic legitimacy of the power at the disposition of transnational enterprises[1], and of the use of such power in their host countries, can be undertaken at increasing levels of complexity. First, economic legitimacy (or non-legitimacy) can be the result of an analysis of the net effects (income, balance of payments, etc.) that are generated by the activities of foreign subsidiaries. Given a firm's resource needs that are created for the continuing expansion of its activities, some of which are geographically concentrated, and also given the existing structural market imperfections, it is quite possible that in some sectors, some countries might register net negative effects even if the net world 'welfare' is positive. The legitimacy, then, of the operations of foreign subsidiaries in these sectors and countries is placed under question.

A second level at which we can analyse legitimacy in the exercise of power refers to the effect that such power has in the distribution of returns among foreign firms and host countries even if both of them have net positive effects. If one applies a benefit–cost analysis, not separately for each one of the participants, but to a project as a whole, the sharing of the returns that are distributable becomes a matter of concern in itself. This is more so since size of returns and their distribution need not be, and often are not, independent of each other. Legitimacy of power becomes, in this case, a matter of relative standing among the participants. Such legitimacy is a function of knowledge of the total size of returns, knowledge of the possible usage of power and its effects on the distributable elements, knowledge of other alternatives offered, etc. Furthermore, legitimacy, being relative at this level, depends on the standing of the participants during previous periods of time as well as on the threshold of their future expectations. In the preceding chapters, we tried to present an analysis of the package of returns that accrue from operations of trans-

---

[1] Economic legitimacy is defined as conformity with the interests of host countries of the net effects inherent in the use of power by transnational enterprises.

national enterprises in developing countries under a market structure characterized by various forms of sequential or interdependent monopolies. (We acknowledge that the findings of our analysis changed progressively our own appreciation of the legitimacy of power of foreign firms in developing countries.)

A third level at which legitimacy of power can be analysed refers, not to the direct measurable effects over a given year, but to the quantifiable and non-quantifiable effects over various periods of time. They, in turn, are related to the effects of foreign subsidiaries in the sustained development of a country. In economic terms such development can be considered with respect to the creation and fomentation of the resource potential of a country, in terms of entrepreneurs, managers, capital, technological capacities, export opportunities, etc. Occasionally effects of policies during a given year, or years, might be positive while in the medium run they could turn negative and vice versa. Did Colombia enhance or endanger its interests by agreeing in the Andean Pact on the principle of progressive national participation in the ownership of foreign subsidiaries? Did Peru gain by the nationalization of the International Petroleum Company? What were the economic effects of the recent policies of Venezuela in curbing part of the power of the foreign oil companies in that country? The questions raised are economic. The answers are given and the decisions are made, but rarely by economists.

Finally, there is a fourth level of analysis on the legitimacy of power enjoyed by foreign firms. It deals with their effects on the structure of societies, on accentuating, or not, class differences, on promoting or blocking social change, on creating or not creating sustained dependence on foreign centres of decisions, etc. Both the questions and the answers at this level are basically political.

# Appendix 1

Clearly for the foreign investor the relevant evaluation of foreign operations is not based on the income and balance sheet statements of the subsidiary, but on the effect that his foreign operations have on the over-all system. Effective profitability for the parent corporation's foreign operations then includes the following:

1. The profits declared by the subsidiary which correspond to financial investment and which constitute actual or potential repatriated dividends.

2. The payments of royalties and/or fixed payments for technical assistance. (In the majority of cases the total amount of these payments constitutes net profit for the parent since the marginal cost of selling an already discovered and developed know-how is zero.[1])

3. The effects of capitalization of know-how.[2] (These effects often constitute a double 'charge' for know-how since the company is already paying royalties for it.) These effects include the following:

   (a) Capitalization enhances the ownership share of the foreign firm while conserving capital. The outcome is certainly critical for joint ventures. The dividend payments accruing to such capital ownership are an implicit (but very real) payment for technology.

   (b) Capitalization of know-how decreases tax payments in the host country through possible depreciation charges of intangible assets.

   (c) In some countries (such as Colombia) tax payments are reduced by enhancing the capital base and thus reducing the factor upon which 'excess profit' tax coefficients[3] are estimated.

   (d) Enhancing the capital base of a firm through know-how also effects the rate at which profits can be repatriated in countries

---

[1] For counterexamples see J. Baranson, 'Technology Transfer Through the International Firm', American Economic Association Meeting, New York, Dec. 1969, p. 5.

[2] See 'Advantages and Problems in Joint Ventures', Harvard Business School, 1964. Also '... in many cases, a substantial part of the U.S. corporation's investment is in the form of capitalized know-how...' Y. Aharoni, *The Foreign Investment Decision Process*, p. 72.

[3] See G. J. Eder, J. C. Chommie, and H. J. Becerra, *Taxation in Colombia*, World Tax Series, Harvard Law School, Cambridge, Mass., 1964.

where such a rate is based upon a company's net foreign capital investment[4] or net worth.

4. The effects of capitalized machinery are equivalent to 3 (a), (b), (c), and (d), described above with reference to capitalized know-how. Quite often such machinery has been completely depreciated in the parent's books and it is not infrequent that its alternative use, outside its scrap value, is very close to zero.[5]

5. One of the most critical benefits derived by a foreign technology and/or capital supplier is that resulting from the creation of a secure market for intermediate products and capital goods. In several cases this benefit is by far the most important one. The benefits derived by the foreign investor from the creation of a secure market for intermediate products can in turn be divided, for policy implications for the host countries, into two parts:

(a) The difference between the incremental cost of producing the intermediate products exported to a developing country and their 'competitive' price in the 'international market', and

(b) The difference between the monopolist price in which these products are sold by the technology and/or capital supplier to the receiver and the 'competitive' price in the international market.

6. Another benefit derived by the technology supplier, a benefit which is not easily quantifiable but which could be of paramount importance in affecting all the other benefits specified above (numbers 1 to 5) is that of control. Although control has been claimed to represent the focus of conflict between supplier and recipient, particularly of capital, it is quite generally identified in a narrow sense and is not pursued beyond the fact (or appearance) of local participation in equity ownership. On the other hand, a substantial degree of control can be exercised over the operations of an enterprise by a foreign supplier of know-how by means implicit in the flow of technology as such (i.e. privileges that stem from the nature of a patent), as well as by explicit arrangements appearing in the agreement of know-how commercialization.

Ownership, defined broadly enough, applies not only to physical or financial assets but also to the right to participate in certain forms of decision-making (i.e. to marketing policies which although contrary to the global interests of a multinational firm are in congruence with those of a particular country), to employment and employment

---

[4] See Colombian Article 116 of Law-Decree 444 of 1967 as amended.

[5] The parent will pay taxes on capital gains, but these taxes are only a fraction of the machinery's new value, while the returns to it, over time, will generally be a multiple of several times the book value. See Y. Aharoni, op. cit., pp. 72–3.

opportunities, to the ability to plan and alter future operations, etc. If the characterizing property of ownership is taken to be the yield of a stream of income to the possessor,[6] then this enlarged definition appears legitimate. Furthermore, if ownership is exercised through the control of the owned entity, then any loss of control results in loss of ownership.[7]

Since whatever consideration 'of a political or economic order'[8] is present in the evaluation of foreign equity participation, as this is exercised in 'controlling policies', similar considerations should be applied in the control resulting from the commercialization of know-how. This gained control should be weighted as part of the effective benefit derived by the technology supplier, and its mirror image (the control lost) as part of the effective cost accruing to the technology purchaser. What are relevant here are not only the 'psychological insecurities'[10] of 'national ideology'[11] and 'fears of foreign domination',[12] but the very real facts of loss of control, which could have overwhelmingly important *economic* repercussions.

7. A further benefit can be derived by the foreign supplier of resources through the use of debt as a substitute for equity participation. (Such arrangement could be advantageous for the repatriation of the principal while repatriation of capital investment might be in some way restricted by the host country.) The interest payments for such debt are an effective benefit for the foreign investor as are his profits.[13]

[6] See H. G. Johnson, 'A Theoretical Model of Economic Nationalism in Developing States', *Political Science Quarterly* (June 1965), p. 176.

[7] As U.S. corporations have discovered in their experience with covenants in their (bank) loans (see Williams, 'Financial Management: Theory and Cases'), equity participation can be reduced to a narrowly defined profit participation which is in turn determined and controlled by the loss of the prerogatives of decision-making through the covenants.

[8] See United Nations, 'Accelerated Flow of Capital and Technical Assistance to the Developing Countries', Feb. 1965, p. 22.

[10] Sidney E. Rolfe, from report on multinational ventures for the U.S. Council, International Chamber of Commerce, *N.Y. Times*, 12 May 1969.

[11] R. Vernon, 'Long Run Trends in Concession Contracts', *American Journal of International Law*, vol. 61 (1967), p. 87.

[12] For comments on this see Jack Baranson, 'U.S. Business in Latin America: A New Approach is Necessary', *Challenge*, Dec. 1962. Also for the fears of 'colonialismo tecnológico' see L. V. Urquidi, 'El Desarrollo Latinoamericano, el Capital Extranjero y la Transmisión de Tecnología', *El Trimestre Económico* (Jan.–Mar. 1962).

[13] If the investment reflects on expansive strategy (as opposed to a defensive one which results from the fear of loss of a market), then from the above benefits one has to subtract the forgone sales of final goods through exports.

# Appendix 2

Let $R$ = Revenue of parent from sales to home market and to non-affiliates abroad.

$C$ = Costs of parent.

$Y$ = Net income of subsidiary which can be declared as profit and, after it has been taxed, it will be remitted to the parent (Case A) or it can be remitted directly through transfer pricing (Case B).

$t$ = Corporate tax rate in country of parent and subsidiary.

$P$ = Profits after taxes of parent firm. ($P^A$ and $P^B$ are after tax profits from Cases A and B respectively.)

1, 2 are subscripts to denote periods one and two.

*Assumption*: Let

$$R_1 < C_1 \tag{1}$$

PERIOD ONE

*Case A*:

$$P_1^A = R_1 + (1 - t)Y_1 - C_1 \tag{2}$$

No taxes will be paid in home country of parent since taxes were paid for $Y_1$ in host country for which a tax credit exists and $R_1 < C_1$.

*Case B*:

$$P_1^B = (1 - t)(R_1 + Y_1 - C_1) \tag{3}$$

If $P_1^A = R_1 + (1 - t)Y_1 - C_1 > 0$ then, as shown in the text,

$$P^A < P^B$$

or

$$R_1 + (1 - t)Y_1 - C_1 < (1 - t))R_1 + Y_1 - C_1)$$

or

$$R_1 - C_1 < (1 - t)(R_1 - C_1) \quad \text{since} \quad R_1 - C_1 < 0$$

*Hence Case B will be preferred* and the difference in after-case profits for the firm between Case B and Case A will be:

$$P^B - P^A = (3) - (1)$$

or

$$P^B - P^A = (1 - t)(R_1 + Y_1 - C_1) - R_1 - (1 - t)Y_1 + C_1$$
$$= -t(R_1 - C_1) \tag{4}$$
$$= (1 - x)Yt \tag{4a}$$

where $(1 - x)$ is the percentage of $Y$ for which no taxes are paid in Case B and $x$ is the percentage where taxes are paid in the same Case.

*Note*:

$$(1 - x)Y_1 = C_1 - R_1 \quad \text{since} \quad R + (1 - x)Y = C$$

Furthermore (4) will represent the global tax savings of the enterprise.

If $R_1 = (1 - t)Y_1 - C_1 < 0$ then there will be a carry-forward in Case A.

For simplicity let us assume that $P_1^B > 0$ so that there is no carry forward from Case B but only from A.

PERIOD TWO

*Case A*: Net income of parent before taxes:

$$R_2 + (1 - t)Y_2 - C_2 \tag{5}$$

Taxable income in home country will

— exclude the profit remissions from subsidiary since they have already been taxed

— include a deduction equivalent to the declared losses carried forward from period one.

Hence taxable income:

$$R_2 - C_2 + \{R_1 + (1 - t)Y_1 - C_1\} \tag{6}$$

Taxes paid at home if (6) > 0:

$$t\{R_2 - C_2 + R_1 + (1 - t)Y_1 - C_1\} \tag{7}$$

$$P_2^A = (5) - (7)$$
$$= R_2 + (1 - t)Y_2 - C_2 - t\{R_2 - C_2 + R_1 + (1 - t)Y_1 - C_1\}$$
$$= (1 - t)(R_2 + Y_2 - C_2) - t\{R_1 + (1 - t)Y_1 - C_1\} \tag{8}$$

*Case B*:

$$P_2^B = (1 - t)(R_2 + Y_2 - C_2) \tag{9}$$

Hence $P_2^A > P_2^B$ by the tax credit from the declared losses in period one which were carried forward.

PERIODS ONE AND TWO TAKEN TOGETHER

$$P_1^A + P_2^A = (2) + (8)$$
$$= R_1 + (1 - t)Y_1 - C_1 + (1 - t)(R_2 + Y_2 - C_2)$$
$$- t\{R_1 + (1 - t)Y_1 - C_1\} \qquad (10)$$
$$= (1 - t)\{R_1 + (1 - t)Y_1 - C_1\} + (1 - t)(R_2 + Y_2 - C_2)$$
$$P_1^B + P_2^B = (3) + (9)$$
$$= (1 - t)(R_1 + Y_1 - C_1) + (1 - t)(R_2 + Y_2 - C_2) \qquad (11)$$

A comparison between Case A and Case B will depend on (10) $\gtreqless$ (11), or after simplifying,

$$(1 - t)\{R_1 + (1 - t)Y_1 - C_1\} \gtreqless (1 - t)(R_1 + Y_1 - C_1)$$

or

$$(1 - t)Y_1 \gtreqless Y_1$$

Since $Y_1 > 0$ and $1 > (1 - t) > 0$, therefore,

$$P_1^A + P_2^A < P_1^B + \tfrac{B}{2}$$

*Hence again Case B will be preferred.* (Our conclusion would have been further strengthened had we taken into account the opportunity cost of money for the tax savings realized in period two.) The difference in after-tax profits for the firm between Case B and Case A will be:

$$P_1^B + P_2^B - P_1^A - P_2^A = (11) - (10)$$
$$= (1 - t)(R_1 + Y_1 - C_1) + (1 - t)$$
$$\times (R_2 + Y_2 - C_2) - (1 - t)\{R_1 + (1 - t)Y_1 - C_1\}$$
$$- (1 - t)(R_2 + Y_2 - C_2)$$
$$= (1 - t)Yt \quad \text{for} \quad Y_1 = Y_2 = Y \qquad (12)$$

(12) represents also the global savings in taxes for the two periods after accounting for the carry-forward tax effect of Case A.

PROOF. (To simplify matters and for consistency with the above let $Y_1 = Y_2 = Y$. This assumption does not alter the meaning of our conclusion.)

*Taxes paid in Case A*

  *Period one*: $tY$ paid by the subsidiary.
  *Period two*: $tY$ paid by the subsidiary.
  $t\{R_2 - C_2 + R_1 + (1 - t)Y - C\}$ paid by the parent as shown in (7) after taking into account the effect of carry-forward from losses declared in period one.
  Total taxes paid in Case A $= T^A$, where

$$T^A = t(3Y + R_2 - C_2 + R_1 - tY - C_1) \qquad (13)$$

*Taxes paid in Case B*

*Period one*: $t(R_1 + Y - C_1)$ paid by the parent.
*Period two*: $t(R_2 + Y - C_2)$ paid by the parent.
Total taxes paid in Case B $= T^B$, where

$$T^B = t(2Y + R_2 - C_2 + R_1 - C_1) \qquad (14)$$

Differences in taxes paid between two cases:

$$T^A - T^B = (13) - (14).$$

After simplifying,

$$T^A - T^B = t(Y - tY) = (1 - t)Yt \qquad (15)$$

As it can be seen, (12) is equal to (15).

*Note*: The effect of carry-forward (or its absence) on the difference on after-tax profits between Cases A and B, other things being equal, will depend on the comparison between $(1 - x)$ and $(1 - t)$ as can be seen, by contrasting equation (4a) $= (1 - x)Yt$ with equation (12) $= (1 - t)Yt$.

# Appendix 3

Suppose a parent corporation:

(a) declares during a given year costs $(C)$ of $180 undertaken for its global operations over time.

(b) obtains revenues $(R_d)$ of $150 from sales to the domestic market and from sales to non-affiliates abroad; and

(c) has an additional income of $100 from the operations of its foreign subsidiaries.

The parent can direct its subsidiaries to declare the $100 as profits in their host countries, pay taxes, and remit the rest at home (Case A). Or the parent can charge its subsidiaries abroad the $100 through higher prices on related interaffiliate sales and declare the income directly at the home country (Case B). If the corporate tax rate at the home country and the rest of the world is 50 per cent and the other assumptions from p. 99 also hold then results will accrue as shown in Table A3. 1.

TABLE A3. 1

| Description of accounting reporting steps | Case A | Case B |
|---|---|---|
| (a) Additional charges claimed by the parent and charged to the foreign subsidiaries | $<br>0 | $<br>100 |
| (b) Profits of subsidiaries before taxes | 100 | 0 |
| (c) Taxes paid in host countries ($100 × 50%) | 50 | 0 |
| (d) Remitted after-tax profits | 50 | 0 |
| (e) Total gross margin of the parent including domestic and foreign activities | ($150 + $50) 200 | ($150 + $100) 250 |
| (f) Costs of the parent | 180 | 180 |
| (g) Profits before taxes by parent ((e) minus (f)) | 20 | 70 |

| | | | |
|---|---|---|---|
| (h) taxes paid in home country | tax credit for payment of taxes abroad | 0 (70 × 50%) | 35 |
| (i) After-tax profits declared in home country | | 20 | 35 |

---

Case A resulted in $20 as after-tax profits for the parents while Case B netted $35. The difference of $15 is due to an over-all tax reduction for the corporation of an equivalent amount. (Taxes in Case A amounted to $50 while in Case B they were $35.) The same net gain through global tax reductions could have been achieved if only a part of the $100 was reported directly as income generated by the parent *as long as* that part covered the difference between the reported costs of the parent and the revenues it obtained from domestic activities and to non-affiliates abroad. This is likely to be the more common case (Case $B_n$) characterizing the operations of transnational corporations, where (some) profits are declared by the parent *and* its subsidiaries. The results of Case $B_n$ are equal to those of Case B and different to those of Case A as long as the following two conditions are met:

$$R_d < C$$

and

charges by the parent on its subsidiaries $\geqslant C - R_d$

Using the same numerical example as in the previous page, Case $B_n$ is shown in Table A3. 2.

TABLE A3. 2

| Description of accounting reporting steps | | Case $B_n$ |
|---|---|---|
| (a) Additional charges claimed by the parent and charged to the foreign subsidiaries: | | $ 40 |
| (b) Profits of subsidiaries before taxes | ($100 − $40) | 60 |
| (c) Taxes paid in host countries | ($60 × 50%) | 30 |
| (d) Remitted after-tax profits | | 30 |
| (e) Total gross margin of the parent including domestic and foreign activities | ($150 + $40 + $30) | 220 |
| (f) Fixed costs of parent | | 180 |

*Note*: The parent charged the subsidiaries $40 out of the possible total of $100, where $40 > $180 − $150 = C. − R_d.

(g) Profits before taxes by parent ((e) minus (f))          40

(h) Taxes paid in home country          Tax credit for the⎫
profits of \$30 out of ⎪
the \$40 for fiscal ⎪
charges paid abroad ⎬          5
and payment of \$10 × ⎪
50% for the remain- ⎪
ing.          ⎭

(i)  After-tax profits declared in home country          35

---

Hence after-tax profits for the parent in Case $B_n$ = those of Case B = \$35 > those of Case A = \$20. Also, global tax payments in Case $B_n$ = those of Case B = \$35 < those of Case A = \$50.

# Appendix 4

Let $R$, $C$, $Y$, $x$, $t$, $t_1$, $t_2$, $p$, and $\tau$ stand as defined in the text and $R - C < 0$ while $R + (1 - t)Y - C > 0$. Also let $P^A$ and $P^B$ stand respectively for profits after taxes of parent firm from Case A (where $Y$ is declared as profit and is being taxed in the host country) and Case B (where $Y$ is transferred to the parent through transfer pricing).

*Tariff levels*

$$t_1 = t_2 = t$$
$$P^A = R + (1 - t)Y - C \tag{1}$$

No taxes are paid in the home country since $R - C < 0$ and $Y$ was taxed in the host countries for which a tax credit is applied. In Case B only a part ($M$) of $Y$ will be remitted through transfer pricing while the other will cover the tariff payments in the host country resulting from the transfer pricing.
Hence

$$M + \tau M = Y \quad \text{or} \quad M = \frac{Y}{1 + \tau} \tag{2}$$

$$P^B = (1 - t)(R + M - C) = (1 - t)\left(R + \frac{Y}{1 + \tau} - C\right) \tag{3}$$

The two cases will be equivalent if $P^A = P^B$ or $(1) = (3)$ or, after simplifying,

$$(1 - t)Y = \frac{(1 - t)Y}{1 + \tau} - t(R - C) \tag{4}$$

According to our definition $(1 - x)$ is the percentage of foreign earned income remitted through transfer pricing to the parent for which no corporate profit taxes are paid since it goes to cover the difference between $R$ and $C$. Hence

$$R - C + (1 - x)M = 0 \quad \text{or, using (2),} \quad R - C + \frac{(1 - x)Y}{1 + \tau} = 0$$

Hence

$$R - C = -\frac{(1 - x)Y}{1 + \tau} \tag{5}$$

Thus (4) becomes

$$(1 - t)Y = \frac{(1 - t)Y}{1 + \tau} + t\frac{(1 - x)Y}{1 + \tau}$$

Re-arranging and solving for $\tau$ we find that the two Cases will be equivalent if

$$\tau = \frac{t(1 - x)}{1 - t} \tag{6}$$

*Tax differentials*

Let $t_1 > t_2$ and $\tau = 0$.

Remitted profits to the parent in Case A: $Y(1 - t_2)$. The relevant tax rate in the home country will be $(t_1 - t_2)$ so as to account for the credit on taxes paid abroad.

Hence, since $R < C$,

$$P^A = \{1 - (t_1 - t_2)\}\{R - C + (1 - t_2)Y\} \tag{7}$$

Also

$$P^B = (1 - t_1)(R - C + Y) \tag{8}$$

The two cases will be equivalent if $(7) = (8)$. After rearranging, simplifying, using $(5)$, and solving for $t_1$ we find that the two cases will be equivalent if

$$t_1 = (1 - x) + t_2 \tag{9}$$

*Tax differentials and tariff rates*

Let $t_1 > t_2$ and $\tau > 0$.

$$P^A = (7)$$

As deduced from $(3)$,

$$P^B = (1 - t_1)(R + \frac{Y}{1 + \tau} - C) \tag{10}$$

The two cases will be equivalent if $(7) = (10)$. By rearranging, simplifying, using $(5)$, and solving for $\tau$ we find that the firm will be indifferent on transfer pricing if

$$\tau = \frac{t_2\{1 - (t_1 - t_2) - x\}}{1 - t_1 + t_2(t_1 - t_2)} \tag{11}$$

*Local participants with zero tariffs*

$$P^A = R + (1 - t)Yp - C = (1 - t)Yp + (R - C) \tag{12}$$
$$P^B = (1 - t)(R + Y - C) = (1 - t)Y + (1 - t)(R - C) \tag{13}$$

Since $0 < p < 1$ and $R - C < 0$, therefore $P^B > P^A$.

*Local participants and positive tariffs*

$$P^A = (12)$$
$$P^B = (3)$$

The two cases will be equivalent if $(12) = (3)$ or

$$R + (1 - t)Y_p - C = (1 - t)(R + \frac{Y}{1 + \tau} - C)$$

or after simplifying and solving for $\tau$ we find that the firm will be indifferent on transfer pricing if

$$\tau = \frac{t(p - x) + (1 - p)}{(1 - t)p} \tag{14}$$

## Appendix 5

PHARMACEUTICAL PRODUCTS

| Product | Quotations of international prices (FOB) U.S. $ | Country | Company | Price of importation in Colombia (FOB) U.S. $ | Over-pricing % |
|---|---|---|---|---|---|
| Chlordiazepoxide (7-chloro-2-methylamino-5-phenyl-3H-1,4-benzodiazepine-4-oxide) | 19·00 kg | West Germany | #1 | 1,250 kg | 6,155 |
|  | 19·50 kg | Italy |  |  |  |
|  | 20·00 kg | West Germany |  |  |  |
|  | 21·00 kg | Italy |  |  |  |
|  | 18·90 kg | Italy |  |  |  |
| Diazepam (7-chloro-1,3-dihydro-1-methyl-5-phenyl-2H-1,4-benzodiazepin-2-one) | 40·00 kg | Italy |  |  |  |
|  | 45·55 kg | West Germany | #2 | 2,500 kg | 6,478 |
|  | 30·00 kg | Italy |  |  |  |
|  | 37·00 kg | Italy |  |  |  |
|  | 36·00 kg | Italy |  |  |  |
|  | 38·00 kg | Italy |  |  |  |

*Note*: Unless otherwise stated, listed prices are 1968 prices.

### Ampicillin (D(2-amino-2-phenylaceamide)-3,3-dimethyl-7-oxo-4-thia-lazabicyclo-(3.2.o)-heptane-2-carboxylicacid)

| Price | Country | Ref. | Quantity | Value |
|---|---|---|---|---|
| 162·50 kg | Italy | | | |
| 177·00 kg | Italy | #1 | 420·00 kg | 136·5 |
| 188·00 kg | Denmark | #2 | 276·80 kg | 55·8 |
| *177·60 kg* | West Germany | | | |
| 200·00 kg | Holland | | | |
| 164·00 kg | Italy | | | |
| 165·00 kg | Italy | | | |
| 190·00 kg | Italy | | | |

### Tetracycline hydrochloride

| Price | Country | Ref. | Quantity | Value |
|---|---|---|---|---|
| *23·00 kg* | Italy | #1 (68) | 180·00 kg | 682·6 |
| 28·75 kg | West Germany | #2 (67) | 250·00 kg | 987 |
| 26·00 kg | West Germany | #2 (68) | 150·00 kg | 552 |
| 22·50 kg | Italy | #2 (69) | 110·00 kg | 378 |
| 26·15 kg | Denmark | #3 | 135·70 kg | 490 |
| 22·50 kg | Portugal | #4 | 130·00 kg | 465 |
| 21·50 kg | Poland | | | |
| 20·50 kg | Yugoslavia | | | |
| 21·50 kg | Spain | | | |
| 21·40 kg | Italy | | | |

### Tetracycline (base)

| Price | Country | Ref. | Quantity | Value |
|---|---|---|---|---|
| 23·50 kg | Italy | #1 (68) | 250·00 kg | 948 |
| *23·85 kg* | Italy | #1 (69) | 110·00 kg | 361 |
| 26·00 kg | West Germany | #2 | 40·90 kg | 71·5 |
| 25·50 kg | Italy | #3 | 33·00 kg | 39 |

| Product | Quotations of international prices (FOB) U.S. $ | Country | Company | Price of importation in Colombia (FOB) U.S. $ | Over-pricing % |
|---|---|---|---|---|---|
| Tetracycline phosphate complex | 23·00 kg | Italy | | | |
| | 26·00 kg | Italy | #1 (67–8) | 250·00 kg | 987 |
| | 21·50 kg | Spain | #1 (69) | 110·00 kg | 378 |
| | 22·00 kg | Italy | | | |
| | 22·50 kg | Italy | | | |
| Erythromycin estolate | 120·00 kg | Italy | | | |
| | 132·00 kg | West Germany | | | |
| | 145·50 kg | Italy | #1 | 275·56 kg | 108·7 |
| | 200·00 kg | Holland | | | |
| | 138·00 kg | Italy | | | |
| | 110·00 kg | Italy | | | |
| | 100·00 kg | Italy | | | |
| Erythromycin ethylsuccinate | | | | | |
| 600 mg/g | 200·00 kg | Italy | #1 | 480·00 kg | 140 |
| 850 mg/g | 275·00 kg | Italy | #1 | 550·00 kg | 100 |

| | | | | | |
|---|---|---|---|---|---|
| Oxytetracycline | 31.75 kg | West Germany | #1 (67) | 147.00 kg | 387.5 |
| | 30.15 kg | Denmark | #1 (68) | 110.00 kg | 264.8 |
| | 25.50 kg | Italy | #1 (69) | 150.00 kg | 397.5 |
| | 25.55 kg | Switzerland | | | |
| | 29.50 kg | Italy | | | |
| | 33.33 kg | West Germany | | | |
| | 34.50 kg | Italy | | | |
| Promethazine | 19.70 kg | Italy | #1 | 140.00 kg | 654.3 |
| (10-(2-dimethylaminopropyl) | 17.75 kg | Italy | #2 | 90.00 kg | 384.9 |
| phenothiazine base) | 18.56 kg | Italy | #1 | 35,000 kg | 233.3 |
| Triamcinolone acetonide | 10,500 kg | France | #2 | 36,000 kg | 242.8 |
| | | | #2 | 48,250 kg | 360 |
| Triamcinolone alcohol | 6,600 kg | Italy | #1 (67) | 24,000 kg | 233.3 |
| | 7,300 kg | France | #1 (68–9) | 12,000 kg | 66.6 |
| | 7,200 kg | Italy | | | |
| Neomycin sulphate | 37.70 kg | Denmark | #1 | 53.00 kg | 40.6 |
| | | | #2 | 225.00 kg | 497 |
| | | | #3 | 47.50 kg | 26 |
| | | | #4 | 45.00 kg | 20 |
| Oxytetracycline hydrochloride | 28.00 kg | Yugoslavia | #1 | 100.00 kg | 257 |
| Chlortetracycline hydrochloride | 30.00 kg | Italy | #1 | 150.00 kg | 400 |
| Oxytetracycline sterile | 50.00 kg | Yugoslavia | #1 | 200.00 kg | 300 |

| Product | Quotations of international prices (FOB) U.S. $ | Country | Company | Price of importation in Colombia (FOB) U.S. $ | Over-pricing % |
|---|---|---|---|---|---|
| Ampicillin sodium inj. st. | 200·00 kg | Holland | #2 | 402·60 kg | 101·3 |
|  | 240·00 kg | Holland | #1 | 450·00 kg | 125 |
| Declomycin hydrochloride | 191·80 kg | West Germany | #1 | 400·00 kg | 108·5 |
| Dihydrostreptomycin sulphate | 27·50 kg | West Germany | #1 | 29·00 kg | 5·4 |
| Streptomycin sulphate | 23·55 kg | Denmark | #1 | 28·00 kg | 18·8 |
|  |  |  | #2 | 28·20 kg | 19·7 |
| Tiamfenicol | 118·00 kg | Italy | #1 | 173·00 kg | 46·6 |
| Chloramphenicol D (—) | 13·50 kg | Italy | #1 | 27·00 kg | 100 |
| Chloramphenicol succinate | 31·90 kg | West Germany | #1 | 60·00 kg | 88 |
| N-(pyrrolidin methyl) tetracycline | 70·00 kg | Italy | #1 | 550·00 kg | 685 |
| Dexamethasone (9-fluoro-11-B-17,21-trihydroxy-16a-methylpregna-1-4-diene-3,20-dione) | 7·75 kg | West Germany |  |  |  |
|  | 7·10 kg | Italy | #1 | 27·50 g | 267 |
|  | 6·90 g | Italy | #2 | 9·98 g | 33 |
|  | 7·50 g | Italy | #3 | 35·00 g | 357 |

| | | | | | |
|---|---|---|---|---|---|
| 21'-Prednisolone Phosphate disodium | 0·62 g | France | #1 | 12·20 g | 1,868 |
| | | | #2 | 0·84 g | 35 |
| Methyldopa | 18·48 kg | U.S.A. | #1 | 80·00 kg | 333 |
| Hexylresorcinol | 28·50 kg | West Germany | #1 | 61·80 kg | 317 |
| Indomethacin | 72·50 kg | Italy | #1 | 640·00 kg | 611 |
| (1(p-chloro benzoyl)-5-methoxy-2-methylindole-3-acetic acid) | 110·00 kg | Italy | #1 | 320·00 kg | 225·5 |
| | 108·00 kg | West Germany | | | |
| | 90·00 kg | Italy | | | |
| | 84·00 kg | Italy | | | |
| | 85·00 kg | Italy | | | |
| Hydrochlorothiazide | 5·20 kg | Italy | #1 | 90·00 kg | 1,630·7 |
| | 6·10 kg | Italy | | | |
| Hydroxocobalamin | 9·00 g | Italy | #1 | 15·95 g | 77·2 |
| Cyanocobalamin | 5·15 g | Italy | #1 | 6·00 g | 16·5 |
| | | Italy | #2 | 7·00 g | 35·9 |
| Thiabendazole | 31·30 kg | Italy | #1 | 35·00 kg | 11·8 |
| Testosteron cyclopentylpropionate | 260·00 kg | Switzerland | #1 | 900·00 kg | 246 |
| Sulphamethizole | 7·00 kg | Denmark | #1 | 17·90 kg | 156 |
| Desoxycorticosterone acetate | 0·46 g | France | #1 | 5·20 g | 1.030 |
| Aminopyrine | 3·03 kg | Switzerland | #1 | 9·50 kg | 214 |
| | | | #2 | 5·10 kg | 68·3 |

| Product | Quotations of international prices (FOB) U.S. $ | Country | Company | Price of importation in Colombia (FOB) U.S. $ | Over-pricing % |
|---|---|---|---|---|---|
| Guanethidine | 190.80 kg | West Germany | #1 | 920.00 kg | 382 |
| Sulphamethoxypyridazine | 6.70 kg | Holland/Italy | #1 | 63.00 kg | 840 |
| Promathazine | 17.75 kg | Italy | #1 | 90.00 kg | 407 |
| | | | #1 | 23.60 kg | 33 |
| | | | #2 | 140.00 kg | 689 |
| Prochlorperazine | 37.50 kg | West Germany | #1 | 375.00 kg | 900 |
| Progesterone | 120.00 kg | France | #1 | 3,652.00 kg | 2,868 |
| Chlorpromazine Hydrochloride | 20.50 kg | Italy | #1 | 200.00 kg | 876 |
| Metronidazole | 11.15 kg | Italy | #1 (67) | 390.00 kg | 3,398 |
| | 11.20 kg | Italy | #1 (68) | 70.00 kg | 528 |
| | | | #1 (69) | 30.00 kg | 169 |
| Prochlorperazine Methansulphonate | 110.00 kg | Italy | #1 (68) | 470.00 kg | 320 |
| | 112.00 kg | Italy | #1 (69) | 380.00 kg | 239 |
| | 117.00 kg | West Germany | | | |
| | 118.00 kg | Italy | | | |

| | | | | | |
|---|---|---|---|---|---|
| Ethionamide | 34·00 kg | Switzerland | #1 | 75·00 kg | 97·4 |
| 2-Ethylthioisonicotinamide | 38·00 kg | Italy | | | |
| | 39·60 kg | Italy | | | |
| | 40·30 kg | West Germany | | | |
| Penicillin G. procaine | 0·018 MU | Holland | #1 | 0·03 MU | 66·7 |
| D-Calcium pantotenate | 3·30 kg | Gov. Agencies | #1 | 12·75 kg | 286 |
| Thiamine hydrochloride | 10·25 kg | West Germany | #1 | 12·75 kg | 24·4 |
| | | | #2 | 13·86 kg | 35·2 |
| Methimazole | 3·72 kg | Denmark | #1 | 132·47 kg | 3,461 |
| Iodochloroxyquinoline | 4·00 kg | Switzerland | #1 | 5·3 kg | 32·1 |
| | | | #2 | 19·65 kg | 391 |
| Cyanocobalamin in gelatin 1% | 9·45 kg | Italy | #1 | 45·00 kg | 376 |
| Ethambutol dihydrochloride | 62·50 kg | Italy | #1 | 110·00 kg | 76 |
| Oxethazaine | 25·00 kg | West Germany | #1 | 325·00 kg | 1,200 |
| Oxazepam | 33·80 kg | West Germany | #1 | 800·00 kg | 2,267 |

RUBBER PRODUCTS

| Product | Quotations in Malaysian Exchange | Price of importation in Colombia | Overpricing |
|---|---|---|---|
| | U.S. $ | U.S. $ | % |
| Standard flat bark crepe | 0·1181 lb. | 0·18 | 52·5 |
| Rubber #5 ribbed smoked | 0·16 lb. | 0·20 | 25 |

ELECTRONICS COMPONENTS

| T.V. products and nomenclature | Quotations of international prices (FOB) | Country | Company | Price of importation in Colombia (FOB) | Over-pricing |
|---|---|---|---|---|---|
| | U.S. $ | | | U.S. $ | % |
| First amplifiers | | | | | |
| European EF 183 | 0·36 | West Germany | #1 | 1·40 | 258 |
| U.S. 4 EH 7 | | | #1 | 0·50 | 23 |
| | | | #3 | 0·39 | 8 |
| | | | #4 | 1·40 | 258 |

| | | | | | | |
|---|---|---|---|---|---|---|
| European | PCF 201 | | | #1 | 0·52 | 33 |
| U.S. | 509·0 | | | #1 | 0·78 | 100 |
| U.S. | EH 7 | | | #1 | 0·61 | 56 |
| European | EF 184 | | | #1 | 0·045 | 15 |
| U.S. | 6 EJ 7 | | | | | |

Second amplifier of IF valves

| | | | | | | |
|---|---|---|---|---|---|---|
| European | EF 183 | 0·36 | West Germany | #1 | 1·00 | 157 |
| U.S. | 4 EH 7 | | | #2 | 0·61 | 69 |
| | | | | #3 | 0·50 | 39 |
| | | | | #4 | 1·00 | 177 |
| European | PCF | | | #1 | 0·52 | 44 |
| U.S. | 201 | | | | | |
| U.S. | 509 | | | #1 | 0·78 | 116 |
| European | EF 184 | | | #1 | 0·39 | 8 |
| U.S. | 6 EJ 7 | | | #2 | 0·48 | 33 |
| | | | | #3 | 0·45 | 25 |

Third amplifier of IF (video) valves

| | | | | | | |
|---|---|---|---|---|---|---|
| European | 6 CB 6 | 0·38 | West Germany | #1 | 0·52 | 26·8 |
| U.S. | PCF | | | #1 | | |
| | 200 | | | | | |
| European | LF 184 | | | #1 | 0·50 | 32 |
| U.S. | 4 EJ 7 | | | #1 | 1·05 | 156 |
| European | EF 184 | | | | | |

| T.V. products and nomenclature | | Quotations of international prices (FOB) U.S. $ | Country | Company | Prices of importation in Colombia (FOB) U.S. $ | Over-pricing |
|---|---|---|---|---|---|---|
| Third amplifier of IF (video) valves—*(cont.)* | | | | | | |
| U.S. | 6 EJ 7 | | | #1 | 0·61 | 60 |
| U.S. | 4 DK 6 | | | #1 | 0·41 | 7 |
| European | PCF 80 | | | #2 | 0·66 | 73 |
| U.S. | 9 A 8 | | | #1 | 0·44 | 15 |
| European | EF 183 | | | | | |
| U.S. | r EH 7 | | | | | |
| | | | | | | |
| Video detectors in transistors | | | | | | |
| European | Diodo | | Netherlands | | | |
| | OA 90 | 0·05 | | #1 | 0·06 | 20 |
| | | | | #2 | 0·08 | 60 |
| | | | | #3 | 0·07 | 40 |
| European | OA 70 | | | #1 | 1·15 | 2,200 |
| U.S. | 93 B 5 2-1 | | | #1 | 0·17 | 240 |

**Video detector in valves**

| | | | | | | |
|---|---|---|---|---|---|---|
| U.S. | IN6o / Diodo | 0·10 | U.S.A. | #1 | 0·15 | 50 |
| U.S. | IN295 / Diodo | | | #1 | 0·80 | 700 |
| N.S. | Diodo | | | #1 | 0·25 | 150 |
| E | PCL 84 | | | #1 | 0·62 | 520 |
| S. | 15 DX 8 | | | | | |

**Video amplifier in valves**

| | | | | | | |
|---|---|---|---|---|---|---|
| .Q. | 8AW8A½ | 0·335 | U.S.A. | #1 | 0·47 | 30 |
| European | PCL 84 | | | #1 | 1·60 | 377 |
| .S. | 15DXB | | | #2 | 0·51 | 52 |
| | | | | #3 | 0·42 | 25 |
| | | | | #4 | 0·67 | 100 |
| | | | | #5 | | |
| .S. | 10LW8 | | | #1 | 0·84 | 150 |
| .S. | ½6JT 8 | | | #1 | 0·95 | 183 |

**Synchronous splitter-valves**

| | | | | | | |
|---|---|---|---|---|---|---|
| European | LCF80 | 0·265 | U.S.A. | #1 | 0·52 | 56 |
| U.S. | 6LN8-½ | | | #1 | | |
| European | PCL 200 | | | #1 | | |
| European | ECH 81 | | | #1 | 3·30 | 1145 |
| U.S. | 6 AJ 8 | | | #2 | 3·60 | 1258 |

| T.V. products and nomenclature | Quotations of international prices (FOB) U.S. $ | Country | Company | Price of importation in Colombia (FOB) U.S. $ | Over-pricing % |
|---|---|---|---|---|---|
| **Synchronous splitter-valves—(cont.)** | | | | | |
| European  ECH 84 | | | #1 | 0·54 | 103 |
| U.S.  6JX8 | | | #2 | 0·59 | 122 |
| U.S.  66 H 8 | | | #1 | 0·78 | 194 |
| U.S.  ½ 6JT8 | | | #1 | 0·95 | 258 |
| **Synchronous amplifier transistors** | | | | | |
| European  AC 125 | 0·16 | Netherlands | #1 | | |
| **Synchronous amplifier-valves** | | | | | |
| European  6KD8 | 0·32 | U.S.A. | #1 | | |
| European  ECH 84 | | | #1 | 0·54 | 68 |
| U.S.  6JX8 | | | #2 | 0·59 | 87 |
| | | | #3 | 0·57 | 78 |

**Vertical oscillator-valves**

|  | Valve |  |  | # |  |  |
|---|---|---|---|---|---|---|
| U.S. | 8AW8A½ | 0·335 | U.S.A. | #1 | 0·50 | 29 |
| European | PCL85 |  |  | #1 | 1·05 | 213 |
| U.S. | 18GV8 |  |  | #2 | 0·54 | 61 |
|  |  |  |  | #3 | 0·60 | 79 |
|  |  |  |  | #3 | 0·68 | 102 |
|  |  |  |  | #4 |  |  |
| U.S. | 6GH8 |  |  | #1 | 0·78 | 132 |
| U.S. | 6FM7 |  |  | #1 | 0·75 | 123 |

**Phase detector-valves**

|  | Valve |  |  | # |  |  |
|---|---|---|---|---|---|---|
| U.S. | Diodo | 0·15 | U.S.A. | #1 | 0·25 | 66 |
| U.S. | 17528 |  |  | #1 | 0·91 | 506 |
| European | PY88 |  |  | #1 | 0·57 | 280 |
| U.S. | 30AE3 |  |  |  |  |  |

**Horizontal oscillator-valves**

|  | Valve |  |  | # |  |  |
|---|---|---|---|---|---|---|
| European | LCF802 | 0·285 | U.S.A. | #1 | 0·49 | 51 |
| U.S. | 6LX8 |  |  |  |  |  |
| European | PCF802 |  |  | #1 | 0·65 | 128 |
| U.S. | 9JW8 |  |  | #2 | 0·63 | 121 |
|  |  |  |  | #3 | 1·75 | 514 |
| European | PCF80 |  |  | #1 | 0·41 | 43 |
| U.S. | 9A8 |  |  | #2 | 0·66 | 131 |
|  |  |  |  | #3 |  |  |

| T.V. products and nomenclature | Quotations of international prices (FOB) U.S. $ | Country | Company | Price of importation in Colombia (FOB) U.S. $ | Over-pricing % |
|---|---|---|---|---|---|
| Horizontal oscillator-valves—(*cont.*) | | | | | |
| U.S. 8FO 7 | | | #1 | 0·61 | 114 |
| U.S. 6FQ7 | | | #1 | 0·55 | 92 |
| | | | | | |
| Frequency automatic control-valves | | | | | |
| European PCL 84 | 0·42 | West Germany | #1 | 0·75 | 141 |
| U.S. 15DX8 | | | #2 | 0·51 | 21 |
| European PCH200 | | | #1 | 0·52 | 68 |
| U.S. 6CH8 | | | #1 | 0·78 | 85 |
| U.S. 6FQ7 | | | #1 | 0·55 | 30 |
| European ECH84 | | | #1 | 0·71 | 69 |
| U.S. 6JX8 | | | | | |
| | | | | | |
| Frequency automatic control-transistors | | | | | |
| European OA202 | 0·36 | | #1 | | |

**Amplifier of horizontal outlet-valves**

| | Valve | Country | | # | | |
|---|---|---|---|---|---|---|
| European | PL 500 | West Germany | 0·60 | #1 | 0·91 | 51 |
| | | | | #2 | 2·95 | 391 |
| | | | | #3 | 0·83 | 38 |
| | | | | #4 | 1·11 | 85 |
| | | | | #5 | 1·07 | 78 |
| U.S. | 38HE7 | | | #1 | 0·80 | 23 |
| U.S. | 38HK7 | | | #1 | 0·91 | 51 |

**First amplifier of IF (audio) valves**

| | Valve | Country | | # | | |
|---|---|---|---|---|---|---|
| U.S. | 6KD8 | U.S.A. | 0·32 | #1 | 0·50 | 56 |
| European | PCL86 | | | #1 | | |
| U.S. | 14GW8 | | | | | |
| U.S. | 4DT6 | | | #1 | 0·78 | 143 |
| European | EBF89 | | | #1 | 1·40 | 337 |
| U.S. | 6DC8 | | | | | |
| U.S. | 10LW8 | | | #1 | 0·84 | 162 |
| European | EF 184 | | | #1 | 0·39 | 21 |
| U.S. | 6EJ7 | | | #2 | 0·84 | 50 |

**Second amplifier of IF (audio) valves**

| | Valve | Country | | # | | |
|---|---|---|---|---|---|---|
| European | LCF 80 | U.S.A. | 0·265 | #1 | 0·50 | 88 |
| U.S. | 6LN8 | | | #1 | | |
| European | PCP 89 | | | #1 | 0·91 | 243 |
| U.S. | ABF11 | | | | | |

| T.V. products and nomenclature | | Quotations of international prices (FOB) U.S. $ | Country | Company | Price of importation in Colombia (FOB) U.S. $ | Over-pricing % |
|---|---|---|---|---|---|---|
| Second amplifier of IF (audio) valves—*(cont.)* | | | | | | |
| European | PCF80 | | | #1 | 0·41 | 54 |
| U.S. | 9A8 | | | | | |
| European | PCL86 | | | #1 | 0·60 | 126 |
| U.S. | 14GW8 | | | #2 | 0·66 | 149 |
| U.S. | 6DT6 | | | #1 | 0·53 | 100 |
| Second amplifier of IF (audio)-transistors | | | | | | |
| European | AF126 | 0·25 | Netherlands | #1 | | |
| Audio amplifier-valves | | | | | | |
| European | EL 184 | 0·32 | U.S.A. | | | |
| U.S. | 6BQ5 | | | #1 | 0·60 | 87 |
| European | PCL 86 | | | #2 | 0·66 | 106 |
| U.S. | | | | #3 | 0·68 | 112 |
| | | | | #4 | 0·54 | 68 |
| | | | | #5 | 2·55 | 696 |

| | | | # | | |
|---|---|---|---|---|---|
| European | PL84 | | #1 | 0·43 | 34 |
| U.S. | 17CU5 | | #1 | 0·40 | 25 |
| U.S. | ABF11 | | #1 | 0·91 | 184 |
| U.S. | 6AG5 | | #1 | 0·53 | 65 |

**Tuner selector**

| | | | # | | |
|---|---|---|---|---|---|
| U.S. | 5·75 | U.S.A. | #1 | 12·00 | 102 |
| European | | | #1 | 7·80 | 35 |
| U.S. | | | #2 | 7·37 | 28 |
| | | | #3 | 7·45 | 29 |
| | | | #4 | 7·70 | 33 |
| | | | #5 | 7·64 | 32 |
| | | | #6 | 8·10 | 40 |

**Flyback**

| | | | # | | |
|---|---|---|---|---|---|
| U.S. | 1·65 | U.S.A. | #1 | 2·15 | 30 |
| | | | #2 | 2·85 | 72 |
| | | | #3 | 4·00 | 142 |
| European | | | #1 | 2·02 | 22 |
| U.S. | | | #2 | 1·80 | 9 |
| | | | #3 | 1·90 | 15 |
| | | | #4 | 3·60 | 118 |
| | | | #5 | 2·25 | 36 |
| | | | #6 | 2·97 | 69 |

| T.V. products and nomenclature | Quotations of international prices (FOB) U.S. $ | Country | Company | Price of importation in Colombia U.S. $ | Over-pricing % |
|---|---|---|---|---|---|
| Screen tube | | | | | |
| European | 9·00 | Holland | #1 | 18·20 | 102 |
| U.S. | | | #1 | 18·00 | 100 |
| | | | #2 | 17·50 | 94 |
| | | | #3 | 19·50 | 116 |
| | | | #4 | 37·68 | 318 |
| | | | | | |
| Deflection yoke | | | | | |
| U.S. | 1·75 | U.S.A. | #1 | 2·93 | 67 |
| | | | #2 | 5·01 | 186 |
| | | | #3 | 8·70 | 397 |
| | | | #1 | 2·08 | 18 |
| | | | #2 | 2·89 | 65 |
| | | | #3 | 2·70 | 54 |
| | | | #4 | 2·97 | 69 |
| | | | #5 | 5·00 | 186 |
| | | | #6 | 8·70 | 397 |
| | | | #7 | 3·60 | 105 |

**Transformer of vertical outlet**

| | | | | | | |
|---|---|---|---|---|---|---|
| U.S. | | 1·45 | U.S.A. | #1 | 1·50 | 3 |
| | | | | #2 | 1·93 | 33 |
| | | | | #3 | 3·00 | 105 |
| | | | | #4 | 3·60 | 148 |
| European | | | | #1 | 1·56 | 7 |
| U.S. | | | | #2 | 1·57 | 8 |

**Mixer oscillator-transistors**

| | | | | | | |
|---|---|---|---|---|---|---|
| European | BF 195 | 0·14 | Netherlands | #1 | | |
| | | | | #1 | 0·45 | 221 |
| U.S. | 25A60 | | | #2 | 0·60 | 328 |

**Mixer oscillator-valves**

| | | | | | | |
|---|---|---|---|---|---|---|
| European | UCH 81 | 0·39 | Netherlands | #1 | 0·48 | 23 |
| European | ECH 81 | | | #2 | 0·40 | 2 |
| U.S. | 6AV8 | | | #3 | 0·42 | 7 |
| | | | | #4 | 0·52 | 33 |
| | | | | #5 | 0·55 | 41 |

**Amplifier of IF- transistors**

| | | | | | | |
|---|---|---|---|---|---|---|
| European | BF 194 | 0·14 | Netherlands | #1 | 0·35 | 150 |
| European | 25A53 | | | #2 | 0·60 | 328 |
| U.S. | | | | | | |

| Radio products and nomenclature | | Quotations of international prices (FOB) U.S. $ | Country | Company | Price of importation in Colombia (FOB) U.S. $ | Over-pricing % |
|---|---|---|---|---|---|---|
| **Amplifier of IF-valves** | | | | | | |
| European | EBF 89 | 0·225 | Netherlands | #1 | 0·33 | 46 |
| U.S. | 6DC8 | | | #2 | 0·35 | 55 |
| | | | | #3 | 0·57 | 153 |
| European | UBF 80 | | | #1 | 0·39 | 73 |
| U.S. | | | | | | |
| **Detector transistors** | | | | | | |
| European | AA119 | 0·05 | Spain | #1 | 0·60 | 1100 |
| U.S. | 25A53 | | | #1 | 0·15 | 200 |
| European | JN60 | | | #1 | 0·09 | 80 |
| European | OA79 | | | | | |
| **Detector-valves** | | | | | | |
| European | EBF 89 | 0·225 | Netherlands | #1 | 0·33 | 46 |
| U.S. | 6DCB | | | #2 | 0·59 | 162 |
| European | UBF 80 | | | #1 | 0·39 | 73 |
| European | ECH 81 | | | #1 | 0·42 | 86 |
| U.S. | 6AJ8 | | | | | |
| European | 6AV6 | | | #1 | 0·76 | 237 |

### Preamplifier-transistors

| | | | | | | |
|---|---|---|---|---|---|---|
| European | 2SB54 | 0·25 | Japan | #1 | 0·60 | 140 |
| European | AC127 | | | #1 | 0·67 | 168 |

### Preamplifier-valves

| | | | | | | |
|---|---|---|---|---|---|---|
| European | ECC83 | 0·31 | Yugoslavia | #1 | 0·34 | 9 |
| U.S. | 12AXT | | | #2 | 0·60 | 93 |
| | | | | #3 | 0·40 | 29 |
| European | UCL82 | | | #1 | 0·47 | 51 |
| U.S. | ECL86 | | | #1 | 0·84 | 170 |
| European | PCF802 | | | | | |
| U.S. | 19VW8 | | | #1 | 0·63 | 103 |

### Outlet amplifier-transistors

| | | | | | | |
|---|---|---|---|---|---|---|
| European | 2SB56 | 0·55 | Japan | #1 | 0·60 | 9 |
| European | AC127 | | | #1 | 0·67 | 21 |

### Outlet amplifier-valves

| | | | | | | |
|---|---|---|---|---|---|---|
| European | L 84 | 0·32 | Yugoslavia | #1 | 0·40 | 25 |
| U.S. | | | | #2 | 0·34 | 6 |
| | | | | #3 | 0·60 | 87 |
| European | UCL 82 | | | #1 | 0·47 | 46 |
| U.S. | | | | #1 | 0·84 | 162 |

| Amplifier products and nomenclature | | Quotations of international prices (FOB) U.S. $ | Country | Company | Price of importation in Colombia (FOB) U.S. $ | Over-pricing % |
|---|---|---|---|---|---|---|
| **Preamplifier-valves** | | | | | | |
| European | ECC83 | | | | | |
| U.S. | 12Ax7 | 0·40 | Netherlands | #1 | 0·80 | 100 |
| | | | | #2 | 0·60 | 50 |
| U.S. | 6AT6 | | | #1 | 0·49 | 22 |
| European | 6SF5 | | | #1 | 0·83 | 107 |
| **Driver-valves** | | | | | | |
| European | ECC84 | | | | | |
| U.S. | 12Ax7 | 0·34 | Czechoslovakia | #1 | 0·60 | 76 |
| | | | | #2 | 0·80 | 135 |
| European | 6AQ8 | | | #1 | 0·84 | 147 |
| **Outlet amplifier-transistors** | | | | | | |
| European | AC 127 | | | | | |
| U.S. | 2N3055 | 0·45 | Netherlands | #1 | 1·00 | 122 |

| Outlet amplifier-valves | | Quotations of international prices (FOB) U.S. $ | Country | Company | Price of importation in Colombia (FOB) U.S. $ | Over-pricing % |
|---|---|---|---|---|---|---|
| European | EL 84 | 0·40 | Netherlands | #1 | 0·60 | 50 |
| U.S. | 6BQS | | | #1 | 1·89 | 350 |
| U.S. | 786 8 | | | #1 | 1·60 | 300 |

| Record-Player components and nomenclature | Quotations of international prices (FOB) U.S. $ | Country | Company | Price of importation in Colombia (FOB) U.S. $ | Over-pricing % |
|---|---|---|---|---|---|
| Two poles motor | | | | | |
| European | 1·44 | Netherlands | #1 | 3·10 | 115 |
| U.S. | | | #1 | 2·80 | 94 |
| | | | #2 | 1·60 | 11 |
| Four poles motor | | | | | |
| European | 1·15 | Netherlands | #1 | 3·75 | 226 |
| U.S. | | | #2 | 5·80 | 404 |
| Plate | | | | | |
| U.S. | 0·21 | U.S.A. | #1 | 0·71 | 238 |
| | | | #2 | 0·75 | 257 |
| European | | | #1 | 0·89 | 323 |
| U.S. | | | #2 | 0·80 | 280 |

| Record-Player components and nomenclature | Quotations of international prices (FOB) U.S. $ | Country | Company | Price of importation in Colombia (FOB) U.S. $ | Over-pricing % |
|---|---|---|---|---|---|
| Phono-captor without needles | | | | | |
| U.S. | 1·05 | U.S.A. | #1 | 1·75 | 66 |
| | | | #2 | 1·40 | 33 |
| European | | | #1 | 2·25 | 114 |
| U.S. | | | #2 | 1·00 | |
| | | | #3 | 2·00 | 90 |
| Record changer axis | | | | | |
| European | 0·305 | Netherlands | #1 | 2·05 | 572 |
| U.S. | | | #2 | 1·58 | 391 |
| U.S. | | | #1 | 0·605 | 98 |
| | | | #2 | 0·61 | 98 |
| Record press | 0·10 | U.S.A. | #1 | 0·25 | 150 |
| | | | #2 | 0·18 | 80 |

Case of mounting
U.S.

|  |  |  |  |
|---|---|---|---|
| | 0·45 | U.S.A. | |
| | | #1 | 0·50 | 11 |
| | | #2 | 0·71 | 57 |
| | | #3 | 1·00 | 122 |

Abbreviations: O.P.D.R. = Oil, Paint & Drug Reporter.
E.C.N. = European Chemical News.
J.Ch.R. = Japan Chemical Review.

CHEMICAL PRODUCTS

| Product | Quotations of international prices (FOB) | Country | Company | Price of importation in Colombia (FOB) | Over-pricing |
|---|---|---|---|---|---|
| | U.S. $ | | | U.S. $ | % |
| Titanium dioxide (Anatase) | 0·33 kg | Japan (J.Ch.R.) | #1 | 0·4399 kg | 33·3 |
| | | | #2 | 0·4532 kg | 37·3 |
| | | | # | 0·4357 kg | 32·0 |
| | | | # | 0·4158 kg | 26·0 |
| Titanium dioxide (Rutile) | 0·35 kg | U.S.A. price imported by other company | #1 | 0·4342 kg | 24·0 |
| | | | #2 | 0·4256 | 21·6 |
| | | | #3 | 0·42 | 20·0 |

| Product | Quotations of international prices (FOB) U.S. $ | Country | Company | Price of importation in Colombia (FOB) U.S. $ | Over-pricing % |
|---|---|---|---|---|---|
| Sodium Hydrosulphite Technical grade | 0.40 kg | Italy | #1 | 0.536 | 34.0 |
| Ammonium sulphate | 30.4 mg | U.S.A. price (E.C.N.) | #1 <br> #2 | 39 Mg <br> 3745 Mg | 28.2 <br> 23.2 |
| Peppermint Essential Oil | 11.55 kg | U.S.A. price (O.P.D.R.) | #1 | 17.61 | 52.46 |
| Nitrocellulose 30% I.P.A. | 0.1726 lb. | U.S.A. price imported by other company | #1 <br> #2 <br> #3 | 0.22 lb <br> 0.22 lb <br> 0.275 lb. | 27.46 <br> 27.46 <br> 59.32 |
| Pentaerythritol technical grade | 0.185 lb. | U.S.A. price imported by other company | #1 <br> #2 <br> #3 | 0.1922 lb. <br> 0.314 lb. <br> 0.19 lb. | 3.9 <br> 69.7 <br> 2.7 |
| Hydroxyethylcellulose | 0.69 lb. | U.S.A. price (O.P.D.R.) | #1 | 0.77 lb. | 11.6 |
| Phosphorous sesquysulphide | 0.38 lb. | U.S.A. price (O.P.D.R.) | #1 | 0.44 | 15.8 |

| | | | | | |
|---|---|---|---|---|---|
| Shellac | 0·968 kg | U.S.A. price (O.P.D.R.) | #1 | 1·30 | 34·3 |
| Phenol U.S.P. Crist. | 0·08 lb. | U.S.A. price (E.C.N.) | #1 | 0·09 lb. | 12·5 |
| 2,4D-(2,4-dichlorophenoxy) acetic acid (technical grade 98–99%) | 0·50 kg | West Germany price imported by other company | #1 #2 | 0·566 kg 0·54 kg | 13·2 8·0 |
| 2-4-5T-(2.4.5-trichlorophenoxy) acetic acid (technical grade 98–99%) | 1·92 kg | West Germany price imported by other company | #1 #2 | 2·30 kg 2·03 kg | 19·8 5·7 |
| Dodecylbenzene (technical grade) | 0·196 kg | U.S.A. price imported by other company | #1 | 0·262 kg | 33·6 |
| N-Butylacrylate (technical grade monomer) | 0·2325 lb. | U.S.A. price | #1 | 0·2775 lb. | 19·35 |
| Vinyl acetate (monomer inhibited) | 0·10 lb | U.S.A. price | #1 #2 | 0·115 lb 0·12 lb | 15·0 20·0 |
| Polyethylene terephtalate (technical grade) | 0·70 kg | Spain price imported by other company | #1 #2 | 0·878 kg 0·903 kg | 25·4 29·0 |
| Pulp wood (decoloured) | 0·148 kg | U.S.A. price (O.P.D.R.) | #1 | 0·1753 kg | 18·44 |

| Product | Quotations of international prices (FOB) | Country | Company | Price of importation in Colombia (FOB) | Over-pricing |
|---|---|---|---|---|---|
| | U.S. $ | | | U.S. $ | % |
| Caprolactam | 0·399 kg | West Germany price imported by other company | #1 | 0·43 kg | 7·76 |
| Bentonite | 0·02375 kg | U.S.A. price | #1 | 0·03975 kg | 67·36 |
| Potassium sulphate | 40 Mg | U.S.A. price (O.P.D.R.) | #1 | 47 Mg | 17·5 |
| Zinc powder | 0·39 kg | U.S.A. price (O.P.D.R.) | #1 | 0·424 | 8·7 |

# Index

(T denotes a reference to a table)